Costing

Workbook

AAT Diploma Pathway Unit 6

David Cox

osborne
BOOKS

Published by Osborne Books Limited
Unit 1B Everoak Estate
Bromyard Road
Worcester WR2 5HP
Tel 01905 748071
Email books@osbornebooks.co.uk
Website www.osbornebooks.co.uk

Design by Richard Holt
Cover image from Getty Images

Printed by the Bath Press, Bath

British Library Cataloguing in Publication Data
A catalogue record for this book is available from the British Library

ISBN 1 905777 06 X

Contents

Acknowledgements

The author wishes to thank the following for their help with the editing and production of the book: Mike Gilbert, Rosemarie Griffiths, Claire McCarthy, Jon Moore and Pineapple Publishing. Special thanks go to Roger Petheram, Series Editor, for reading, checking and advising on the development of this workbook.

The publisher is indebted to the Association of Accounting Technicians for its generous help and advice to our author and editors during the preparation of this text, and for permission to reproduce assessment material which has formed the basis for practice Examination tasks in this text.

Author

David Cox has more than twenty years' experience teaching accountancy students over a wide range of levels. Formerly with the Management and Professional Studies Department at Worcester College of Technology, he now lectures on a freelance basis and carries out educational consultancy work in accountancy studies. He is author and joint author of a number of textbooks in the areas of accounting, finance and banking.

Introduction

Costing Workbook is designed to be used alongside Osborne Books' *Costing Tutorial* and is ideal for student use in the classroom, at home and on distance learning courses. Both the Tutorial and the Workbook are written for students preparing for assessment on for Unit 6 'Recording and analysing costs and revenues'.

Costing Workbook is divided into two sections: Workbook Activities and Practice Examinations.

Workbook Activities

Workbook activities are self-contained exercises which are designed to be used to supplement the activities in the tutorial text. A number of them are more extended than the exercises in the tutorial and provide useful practice for students preparing for the Examination.

Practice Examinations

Osborne Books is grateful to the AAT for their kind permission for the reproduction of the AAT Specimen Examination in this section and selected tasks from other Examinations.

answers

The answers to the tasks and exams in the *Workbook* are available in a separate *Tutor Pack*. Contact the Osborne Books Sales Office on 01905 748071 for details or obtain an order form from www.osbornebooks.co.uk.

www.osbornebooks.co.uk

Visit the Osborne Books website, which contains Resources sections for tutors and students. These sections provide a wealth of free material, including downloadable documents and layouts and assistance with other areas of study.

Workbook activities

This section contains activities which are suitable for use with the individual chapters of *Costing Tutorial* from Osborne Books.

1 AN INTRODUCTION TO COST ACCOUNTING

1.1   (a)   Distinguish between cost units and cost centres.

      (b)   Suggest one cost unit and two cost centres for:
- a firm of accountants
- a parcel delivery company

1.2   Suggest likely cost centres for each of the following:

A theatre in a provincial town, where touring productions are staged. The theatre has a bar and a confectionery counter. Ticket sales are dealt with by the theatre's own box office, and the plays are advertised locally.

A garage, which sells new and used cars of two different makes. Cars are also repaired, serviced and valeted.

1.3   The following cost codes are used by Proton Products Limited:
- factory, 200
- office, 250
- depreciation, 700

State the codes that will be used to charge depreciation to:

(a)   the factory cost centre

(b)   the office cost centre

1.4   The following are items of expenditure incurred in a company which manufactures clothing. Sort them and enter them into three columns, headed 'Materials costs', 'Labour costs', and 'Expenses'.

(a)   Cost of insurance of buildings

(b)   Salaries of the office staff

(c)   Cost of zip fasteners

(d)   Cost of electricity

(e)   Wages of storekeepers

(f)   Overtime payments for machinists

(g)   Cost of a consignment of blue denim

(h)   Cost of pre-printed stationery

(i)   Cost of television advertising

(j)   Cost of cones of thread

(k)   Road fund licences for vehicles

(l)   Canteen chef's wages

1.5 Which one of the following is normally classed as a fixed cost for a manufacturing business?

(a) raw materials to make the product

(b) salaries of maintenance staff

(c) production workers paid on the basis of work done

(d) royalties paid to the designer of the product

Answer (a) or (b) or (c) or (d)

1.6 Which one of the following is normally classed as a variable cost for a 'high street' printing shop?

(a) supervisor's salary

(b) rent of shop

(c) electricity used

(d) cost of paper

Answer (a) or (b) or (c) or (d)

1.7 The following figures relate to the accounts of Manley Manufacturing Limited for the year ended 31 December 2007:

	£
Raw materials used in factory	75,280
Wages of production workers	69,180
Salaries of maintenance staff	30,950
Royalties paid to designer of product	15,110
Depreciation of factory plant and machinery	5,000
Electricity	4,160
Rent and rates	10,290
Salaries of office staff	38,450
Depreciation of office equipment	2,400
Sundry factory expenses	3,020
Sundry office expenses	1,590
Sales revenue	315,840

You are to:

(a) Prepare a total cost statement for the year which shows:

- prime cost
- production cost
- total cost

Discuss any assumptions that you make and state if you need further information from the company.

(b) Prepare a profit statement for the year (on the assumption that all the goods manufactured have been sold).

Note: please see the Appendix (page 146) for specimen formats of a total cost statement and a profit statement.

1.8 Bunbury Buildings Limited makes garages and garden sheds which are pre-fabricated as a 'flat pack' in the factory to customer specifications.

You are working in the costing section of Bunbury Buildings and are asked to analyse the following cost items for May 2007 into the appropriate column and to agree the totals:

COST ITEM	TOTAL COST £	PRIME COST £	PRODUCTION OVERHEADS £	ADMIN COSTS £	SELLING AND DISTRIBUTION COSTS £
Wages of employees working on pre-fabrication line	19,205				
Supervisors' salaries	5,603				
Materials for making pre-fabricated panels	10,847				
Cleaning materials for factory machinery	315				
Hire of specialist equipment for one particular job	454				
Sundry factory expenses	872				
Salaries of office staff	6,091				
Repairs to sales staff cars	731				
Depreciation of office equipment	200				
Magazine advertising	1,508				
Sundry office expenses	403				
Hire of display stands used at garden centres	500				
Office stationery	276				
TOTALS	47,005				

2 MATERIALS COSTS

2.1 (a) Suggest:

- two ordering costs
- two stock holding costs

for an organisation that holds a stock of stationery for its own use.

(b) Calculate the Economic Order Quantity (EOQ) from the following information for boxes of 500 C5 envelopes:

- annual usage   200 boxes
- ordering cost   £30.00 per order
- stock holding cost   £1.20 per box per year

Note:

The formula for EOQ is

$$\sqrt{\frac{2 \times \text{annual usage} \times \text{ordering cost}}{\text{stock holding cost}}}$$

2.2 (a) Explain the principles of Just-In-Time (JIT) delivery systems and give one example for a manufacturing business and one example for a service business.

(b) What are the factors that a business or organisation should consider before using JIT for delivery of its purchases from suppliers?

2.3 You are providing accounting help to a friend, Caryl Jones, who has recently set up in business making garden seats and tables. She understands the need to keep records of the different types of timber she has in stock. She has heard of the terms 'first in, first out' and 'last in, first out'; however, she thinks they refer to the physical movement of stock and are not relevant to the pricing of issues to production.

You are to explain by means of a memorandum:

- why FIFO and LIFO are used to price issues of materials
- whether or not FIFO and LIFO relate to the physical movement of stock

2.4 The supplies department of Peoples Bank has the following movements of an item of stock for June 2007:

		units	cost per unit £	total cost £
1 June	Balance	2,000	2.00	4,000
15 June	Receipts	1,800	2.50	4,500
21 June	Issues	3,000		

You are to complete the following table for FIFO and LIFO:

DATE 2007	DESCRIPTION	FIFO £	LIFO £
21 June	Total issue value		
30 June	Total closing stock value		

2.5 Wyezed Limited manufactures a product using two types of materials, Wye and Zed. The accounting policy of the company is to issue material Wye to production using a FIFO basis, and material Zed on a LIFO basis.

The following are the stock movements of materials during the month of August 2007:

Material Wye – FIFO basis

2007		units	cost per unit £
1 Aug	Balance	5,000	5.00
10 Aug	Receipts	2,000	5.25
18 Aug	Receipts	3,000	5.50
23 Aug	Issues	8,000	

Material Zed – LIFO basis

2007		units	cost per unit £
1 Aug	Balance	10,000	4.00
6 Aug	Receipts	5,000	4.20
19 Aug	Receipts	6,000	4.40
24 Aug	Issues	12,000	

(a)   You are to complete the stores ledger records, below, for material Wye and material Zed.

STORES LEDGER RECORD Material Wye								
Date	Receipts			Issues			Balance		
2007	Quantity	Cost	Total Cost	Quantity	Cost	Total Cost	Quantity	Cost	Total Cost
		£	£		£	£		£	£
1 Aug	Balance						5,000	5.00	25,000
10 Aug	2,000	5.25	10,500						
18 Aug	3,000	5.50	16,500						
23 Aug									

STORES LEDGER RECORD Material Zed								
Date	Receipts			Issues			Balance		
2007	Quantity	Cost	Total Cost	Quantity	Cost	Total Cost	Quantity	Cost	Total Cost
		£	£		£	£		£	£
1 Aug	Balance						10,000	4.00	40,000
6 Aug	5,000	4.20	21,000						
19 Aug	6,000	4.40	26,400						
24 Aug									

(b)   At 31 August 2007, the net realisable value of each type of stock is:

- material Wye   £10,000
- material Zed   £44,000

Show the amount at which stocks should be valued on 31 August 2007 in order to comply with standard accounting practice.

2.6   Wyevale Tutorial College is a private college which runs courses for local companies on business and management subjects. The stocks of paper used for photocopying course material are maintained on a FIFO basis at present. The College's accountant has suggested that a change should be made to the LIFO basis.

As an accounts assistant you have been asked to prepare information based on the stock movements of photocopying paper for February 2007 which are as follows:

1 February	Opening stock	100 reams* at £2.10 per ream
5 February	Issues	80 reams
10 February	Purchases	150 reams at £2.20 per ream
15 February	Issues	90 reams
18 February	Purchases	200 reams at £2.25 per ream
24 February	Issues	120 reams

* a ream is 500 sheets

You are to:

(a)   Complete the stores ledger record shown (see next page) for February, using the FIFO basis.

(b)   Calculate the closing stock value at 29 February 2007 using FIFO and LIFO, and then complete the following table:

Method	Closing stock valuation		
	Quantity (reams)	Cost (£)	Total Cost (£)
FIFO			
LIFO			

Date	Receipts			Issues			Balance		
2007	Quantity	Cost £	Total Cost £	Quantity	Cost £	Total Cost £	Quantity	Cost £	Total Cost £
1 Feb	Balance						100	2.10	210

STORES LEDGER RECORD

Photocopying paper (reams)

(c) Write a short memorandum on behalf of the accountant, which explains the difference between the FIFO and LIFO methods of stock valuation. The memorandum will be circulated to members of the College's Finance Committee for discussion and should include your recommendation of the method to be used to ensure that the courses run by the College are not undercosted.

2.7 Go Games Limited sells computer games. At the end of the financial year, the company's stocks include:

300 copies of 'X1X' game that cost £40 each and will sell at only £30, because it is an out-of-date version.

260 copies of a newly-released game, 'X-TRA-G' that cost £56 each and will be sold for £90 each.

100 copies of a current version of 'X-TREME 2' game, which is expected to be up-dated for 'X TREME 3' in the near future. These cost £35 each and normally sell for £55, but because they may soon be out of date, Go Games Limited has reduced the price to £42 each.

You are to:

Calculate the total value of the stock items described above, in order to comply with standard accounting practice.

2.8 A football club shop holds stocks of replica club strip as well as other goods and clothing. The club strip has recently been changed and the old version will have to be sold at greatly reduced prices. At the end of the financial year, the stocks in the shop include:

	Cost	Net realisable value
	£	£
Replica strip (old version)	3,800	2,500
Replica strip (new version)	8,400	11,000
	12,200	13,500

You are to:

Determine the total value of the stock items above, in order to comply with standard accounting practice.

2.9 SummerDaze Limited manufactures plastic garden furniture. Its best seller is the 'Calypso' seat made from white plastic.

The company uses the first in, first out (FIFO) method for valuing issues of materials to production and stocks of materials.

As an accounts assistant at SummerDaze you have been given the following tasks.

Task 1

Complete the following stores ledger record for white plastic for April 2007:

STORES LEDGER RECORD

Product: **White plastic**

Date	Receipts			Issues			Balance	
	Quantity kgs	Cost per kg £	Total Cost £	Quantity kgs	Cost per kg £	Total Cost £	Quantity kgs	Total Cost £
2007								
Balance at 1 April							20,000	20,000
7 April	10,000	1.10	11,000				30,000	31,000
12 April				25,000				
20 April	20,000	1.20	24,000					
23 April				15,000				

Task 2

All issues of white plastic are for the manufacture of the 'Calypso' seat. The following cost accounting codes are used to record materials costs:

code number	description
2000	stock of white plastic
2100	work-in-progress – Calypso seats
3000	creditors/purchases ledger control

Complete the following table, including the cost accounting codes, to record separately the two purchases and two issues of white plastic in the cost accounting records.

2007	Code	Debit	Credit
7 April			
7 April			
12 April			
12 April			
20 April			
20 April			
23 April			
23 April			

2.10 Barkla Bakery Limited makes fruit cakes which are sold to supermarket chains.

You are an accounts assistant at the bakery; your duties include keeping the records of materials stocks up-to-date.

Task 1

Please refer to the stores ledger record shown on page 20.

- You are to complete the stores ledger record using the information from the materials documentation below and on the next page. You will need to identify and apply the stock valuation method in use. Note that VAT is not entered in the cost accounting records.

- Calculate the balance of stock at the close of the week ending 6 August 2007. Note that it is company policy for returns from production cost centres to stores to be valued at the price of the most recent batch issued from stores.

Task 2

Please refer to the materials requisition and the materials returned documentation below and on the next page.

- You are to complete the column headed 'For cost office use only' on each of these two documents.

MATERIALS REQUISITION

Department: Baking

Document no: MR 112

Date: 5 August 2007

Code no	Description	Quantity	For cost office use only *Value of issue (£)*
DMF	Dried mixed fruit	330 kgs	

Authorised by: *Jan Borthwick*   Received by: *J Trebah*

MATERIALS RETURNED

Department: Baking

Document no: MRN 41

Date: 4 August 2007

Code no	Description	Quantity	**For cost office use only** *Value of return (£)*
DMF	Dried mixed fruit	10 kgs	

Authorised by: *Jan Borthwick*

Received by: *J Trebah*

SALES INVOICE
Fruit 'n Nuts Limited
222 Durning Road
Chapeltown TR10 0UP

Invoice to:

Barkla Bakery Limited

Porth Road

Perranville

TR5 8TZ

VAT Registration:	136 2496 82
Date/tax point:	6 August 2007
Invoice number:	4567
Your order number:	821

Description	Total (£)
Dried mixed fruit: 400 kgs at £0.62 per kg	248.00
Goods total	248.00
VAT at 17.5%	43.40
Total due	291.40

Terms: net 30 days

BARKLA BAKERY LIMITED

Checked against document number *GRN 531*

Date received *6 August 2007*

Signed *J. Trebah*

STORES LEDGER RECORD

Product: Dried mixed fruit

Reference: DMF

Date	Receipts				Issues				Balance		
	Document number	Quantity kgs	Cost per kg £	Total Cost £	Document number	Quantity kgs	Cost per kg £	Total Cost £	Quantity kgs	Cost per kg £	Total Cost £
2007											
Balance at 1 August									200	0.50	100.00
									300	0.55	165.00
									500		265.00
2 August					109	150	0.50	75.00	50	0.50	25.00
									300	0.55	165.00
									350		190.00
3 August	524	500	0.60	300					50	0.50	25.00
									300	0.55	165.00
									500	0.60	300.00
									850		490.00

3 LABOUR COSTS

3.1 Briefly describe *three* sources that are used to gather information about work done in order to make payment to employees.

3.2 Clock cards are used to calculate:

(a)   the wages of employees who work on piecework

(b)   the cost of direct materials

(c)   the salaries of monthly paid employees

(d)   the wages of hourly paid employees

Answer (a) or (b) or (c) or (d)

3.3 HSB Mouldings Limited makes cases for television sets at its modern purpose-built factory. The company uses standard hours produced to measure its labout output.

You are to explain what is meant by a standard labour hour produced.

3.4 An employee makes 160 units of product Exe, 100 units of product Wye, and 250 units of product Zed. The standard labour time allowance per unit is: Exe 5 minutes; Wye 6 minutes; Zed 4 minutes.

What is the number of standard labour hours produced?

(a)   24

(b)   35

(c)   40

(d)   44

Answer (a) or (b) or (c) or (d)

3.5 Renne Limited pays its employees on a time rate, with a rate per hour for a 35-hour week. There are two overtime rates: time-and-a-third for weekdays (rate 1), and time-and-a-half for weekends (rate 2). The details of three employees for last week are as follows:

Employee	Time rate per hour	Total hours worked	Overtime rate 1 (hours)	Overtime rate 2 (hours)
L Constantinou	£ 8.70	40	3	2
H Gunther	£ 9.00	38	–	3
J White	£10.20	42	5	2

You are to calculate how much each employee earned for the week.

3.6 Elend Limited, a manufacturing company, pays its production-line employees on a piecework basis, but with a guaranteed time rate. The details of three employees for last week are as follows:

Employee	Time rate per hour	Hours worked	Production	Piecework rate
J Daniels	£10.00	38	800 units	45p per unit
L Ho	£9.50	35	650 units	55p per unit
T Turner	£9.75	36	500 units	73p per unit

You are to calculate how much each employee earned for the week.

3.7 Brock and Company, a manufacturing business, pays its production-line employees on a time basis. A bonus is paid where production is completed faster than the standard hour output; the bonus is 50 per cent of the standard hours saved and is paid at the actual labour rate per hour. The details of four employees for last week are as follows:

Employee	Time rate per hour	Hours worked	Standard hour output	Actual production
H Hands	£10.50	35	50 units	1,950 units
A Khan	£11.75	37	60 units	2,200 units
T Shah	£11.00	38	50 units	2,000 units
D Smith	£10.80	40	60 units	2,490 units

Note: there were no overtime payments last week.

You are to calculate how much each employee earned for the week.

3.8   Harts Doors and Windows Limited is a manufacturer of double-glazed doors and windows. The company has three production departments – cutting, assembly, and finishing. Data relating to labour for a four-week period is given on the labour cost sheet below.

The company uses a bonus scheme whereby employees receive 50 per cent of the standard hours saved in each department paid at the actual labour rate per hour. This is not included in the actual wages cost (below), which shows actual hours multiplied by the actual wage rate. There have been no overtime payments.

LABOUR COST SHEET for the four weeks ended 26 March 2007			
	CUTTING	**ASSEMBLY**	**FINISHING**
Actual wages cost (£)	6,210	4,214	2,268
Standard hours	556	420	290
Actual hours	540	430	270
Standard hours saved			
Bonus (£)			
Total labour cost (£)			

You are to calculate the total labour cost for each department.

3.9   The production manager at Chucky Chicken Limited, which produces ready-to-cook chicken dishes, has been talking with the accountant (your boss) about the possibility of introducing a system of bonus payments for production-line employees.

The accountant has asked you to draft a memorandum addressed from her to the production manager which sets out the merits of a bonus system for both the company and its employees.

3.10   You are an accounts assistant at Three Oaks Printing Company. One of your tasks is to deal with aspects of the company's payroll. The following queries on this week's payroll have been left for you by the book-keeper:

(a)   We paid £400 as overtime to the production-line employees. Should this be treated as a direct or an indirect cost?

(b)   There was a machine breakdown in the binding department. As a consequence, production-line employees, who are normally paid on a piecework basis, were paid the time rate for the period of the stoppage, totalling £150. Should this be treated as a direct cost or an indirect cost?

3.11 SummerDaze Limited manufactures plastic garden furniture. Its best seller is the 'Calypso' seat made from white plastic. The payroll for the week ended 18 June 2007 has been completed, with the following amounts to pay:

		£
•	net wages to be paid to employees	8,000
•	income tax and National Insurance Contributions (NIC) to be paid to the Inland Revenue	1,650
•	pension contributions to be paid to the pension fund	850
	TOTAL PAYROLL FOR THE WEEK	10,500

The total payroll for the week is analysed as:

		£
•	direct labour costs	7,750
•	indirect labour costs	1,500
•	administration labour costs	1,250
		10,500

As an accounts assistant at SummerDaze you have been given the following tasks:

Task 1

Prepare wages control account for the week ended 18 June 2007:

Dr	Wages Control Account	Cr
£		£

Task 2

All of the direct labour costs are for the manufacture of 'Calypso' seats. The following cost accounting codes are in use to record labour costs:

code number	description
2100	work-in-progress: Calypso seats
2200	production overheads
2300	non-production overheads: administration
3100	wages control

Complete the table below to show how the total cost of the payroll is split between the various cost centres of the business.

2007	Code	Debit	Credit
18 June	2100		
18 June	3100		
18 June	2200		
18 June	3100		
18 June	2300		
18 June	3100		

3.12 Perran Limited manufactures surf boards. The following data relates to the production of its 'Porth' brand of board for February 2007:

Total direct labour hours worked	3,000 hours
Normal time hours	2,600 hours
Overtime hours	400 hours
Normal time rate per hour	£10 per hour
Overtime premium per hour	£5 per hour

In the company's cost book-keeping system all direct labour overtime payments are included in direct costs.

The following cost accounting codes are in use to record labour costs:

code number	description
2100	work-in-progress: 'Porth' boards
4400	wages control

You are to:

• calculate the total cost of direct labour for February

• show the cost book-keeping entries, together with account codes, in order to transfer the direct labour costs to work-in-progress

4 EXPENSES

4.1 Terry Hands works for Acme Builders as a member of the direct labour force. However, he has spent the last two weeks re-decorating the company's offices.

How should his wages for this period be dealt with in the accounts? Why is this?

4.2 Classify the following costs (tick the appropriate column):

	capital expenditure	revenue expenditure
(a) building an extension to the administration office		
(b) cleaning materials for factory machinery		
(c) repair of office photocopier		
(d) directors' salaries		
(e) carriage inwards on new machinery		
(f) carriage inwards on raw materials		
(g) installation of computer system		
(h) insurance of computer system		
(i) installation of special wiring for computer system		

4.3 Classify the following costs (tick the appropriate column):

	DIRECT EXPENSES	INDIRECT EXPENSES	
		production overheads	non-production overheads
(a) royalties paid to designer of product			
(b) straight-line depreciation of factory machinery			
(c) office electricity			
(d) insurance of factory buildings			
(e) advertising			
(f) rent on factory			
(g) units of output depreciation of factory machinery			
(h) factory manager's car expenses			
(i) sales department administration			

4.4 Jarvis Trading Limited depreciates its vehicles at 25 per cent per year, using the reducing balance method.

A car for the sales department was bought on 1 January 2007 at a cost of £16,000.

You are to calculate the depreciation amounts for 2007, 2008 and 2009, and to show the residual value at 31 December 2009. (Note: the company's financial year end is 31 December.)

4.5   Cradley Castings Limited has recently bought a new casting machine for which the details are as follows:

CASTING MACHINE

Cost price on 1 January 2007	£20,000 (net of VAT)
Estimated life	4 years
Estimated production:	
2007	55,000 units
2008	50,000 units
2009	40,000 units
2010	35,000 units
Estimated scrap value at 31 December 2010	£2,000 (net of VAT)

The accountant is unsure whether to depreciate the machine using:

- the straight-line method

- the units of output method

She asks you to calculate the depreciation amounts for each year using the two methods. (Note: the company's financial year end is 31 December.)

Explain whether the depreciation amounts will be listed as direct expenses or indirect expenses.

4.6   The production manager of 'Print 'n Go', a specialist short-run printing business, is considering the purchase of a new computer-linked scanner. The cost is likely to be £18,000 (net of VAT) and the scanner will have a life of approximately four years, after which it will have a trade-in value of between £2,000 and £2,500 (net of VAT). The production manager knows from past experience that such equipment has the most use, and will lose most value, in the early part of its life.

As an accounts assistant you are to write a memorandum (on the next page) to the production manager detailing:

- the method of depreciation that could be used

- an approximate rate that could be applied, showing appropriate workings

- reasons for the choice of depreciation method

MEMORANDUM

To:

From:

Date:

4.7   Greenacres Limited manufactures two types of garden lawnmower – the 'Alpha', an electric mower, and the 'Beta', a petrol mower. The general expenses account for the month ended 30 November 2007 has a debit balance of £34,500. This balance is analysed as:

		£
•	direct expenses – Alpha	8,390
•	direct expenses – Beta	6,240
•	production overheads	13,850
•	non-production overheads – selling and distribution	3,170
•	non-production overheads – administration	2,850
		34,500

The following cost accounting codes are in use to record expenses:

code number	description
1500	work-in-progress: Alpha
1600	work-in-progress: Beta
2000	production overheads
2500	non-production overheads: selling and distribution
2600	non-production overheads: administration
3000	general expenses

As an accounts assistant at Greenacres Limited you have been given the following tasks:

Task 1

Prepare general expenses account for the month ended 30 November 2007:

Dr		General Expenses Account			Cr
2007		£	2007		£
30 Nov	Balance b/d	34,500			

Task 2

Complete the following table to show how the total cost of general expenses is split between work-in-progress, production overheads and non-production overheads.

2007	Code	Debit	Credit
30 Nov	1500		
30 Nov	3000		
30 Nov	1600		
30 Nov	3000		
30 Nov	2000		
30 Nov	3000		
30 Nov	2500		
30 Nov	3000		
30 Nov	2600		
30 Nov	3000		

4.8   In the graphs below, draw in the lines to show how fixed costs and variable costs behave with changes in the level of activity.

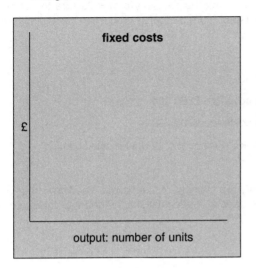

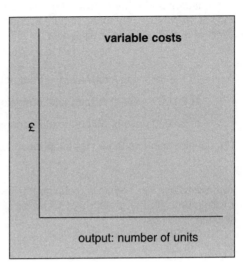

4.9   Classify the following costs (tick the appropriate column):

		FIXED	SEMI-VARIABLE	VARIABLE
(a)	rent of business premises			
(b)	week's hire of machinery at £100 per week for one particular job			
(c)	photocopier with a fixed rental and a cost per unit			
(d)	supervisor's wages			
(e)	reducing balance depreciation			
(f)	production-line employees paid a basic wage, with a bonus linked to output			
(g)	royalty paid to author for each book sold			
(h)	accountant's fees			
(i)	raw materials used in production process			

4.10 The research and development department of Castlemayne Limited, a design and engineering business, has recently developed a new type of electronic dispenser for serving exact quantities of beers, lagers and other drinks. The company has taken the decision to manufacture the product and you are helping the management accountant to prepare budgeted production costs at different levels of output of the new dispenser.

You have the following information in front of you:

- at 20,000 units of output, total budgeted costs are £350,000

- at 30,000 units of output, total budgeted costs are £500,000

The development manager has telephoned to ask the amount of budgeted fixed costs.

You are to use the 'high/low' technique to identify the element of fixed costs. You know from your involvement with the project that variable costs have a linear relationship, and that there are no stepped fixed costs.

4.11 David Khan is a motor vehicle engineer who has designed a fuel pump which gives cars greater fuel economy. He has decided to set up in business to manufacture the product and has carried out market research which suggests that demand for the product will be between 12,000 and 20,000 units each year.

David has budgeted the production costs on the basis of an output of 12,000 units as follows:

			£
variable costs	–	materials	36,000
	–	labour	24,000
	–	expenses	6,000
fixed costs	–	labour	18,500
	–	overheads	25,250

David asks you to prepare a schedule of budgeted production costs based on outputs of 12,000 units, 15,000 units and 20,000 units each year. The schedule is to show total production cost and the cost per unit at each level of output. (Note: you may assume that there is a linear relationship for variable costs, and that there are no stepped fixed costs.)

Briefly describe and explain the trend in costs per unit for the three budgeted levels of production.

5 OVERHEADS

5.1 Mereford Management College is a private college that has two teaching departments – accountancy and management.

The College charges overheads on the basis of lecturer hours. The following overhead analysis information is available to you (note that support services overheads – such as the administration office, reprographics department and learning resources – have already been apportioned to the teaching departments):

OVERHEAD ANALYSIS SHEET for January 2007		
	Accountancy Department	Management Department
Budgeted total overheads (£)	22,143	17,251
Budgeted lecturer hours	1,525	1,300
Budgeted overhead absorption rate (£)		

Details of a particular course – 'Finance for Managers' – that is taught in both the accountancy and management departments are as follows:

OVERHEAD ANALYSIS SHEET Course: Finance for Managers		
	Accountancy Department	Management Department
Lecturer hours	45	20
Budgeted overhead absorption rate (£)		
Overhead absorbed by course (£)		

You are to:

(a) calculate the overhead absorption rate for each of the two departments and complete the overhead analysis sheet

(b) calculate the overhead absorbed by the 'Finance for Managers' course and complete the course overhead analysis sheet

(c) suggest an alternative overhead absorption rate that the College might use and comment on the circumstances that would make it appropriate

5.2 Wyevale Processing Limited processes and packs fruit and vegetables for supermarkets. The company has five departments – processing, packing, quality assurance, stores and maintenance.

The cost accountant has given you an overhead analysis schedule (see next page) to complete for next month.

The following information is available:

	Processing	Packing	Quality Assurance	Stores	Maintenance
Floor area (square metres)	160	210	50	80	100
Employees (number)	10	14	2	2	2
Machine usage (hours)	300	100	40		
Materials requisitions (number)	50	60	12		5
Maintenance hours (number)	60	50	20		

You are to:

(a) Prepare an analysis of budgeted production overheads for next month showing the basis of apportionment to the five departments of the business.

(b) Outline what now needs to be done with the budgeted costs of the service departments in order to arrive at overhead absorption rates for the production departments. Explain the reasons for this action.

5.3 Mercia Metals Limited is a manufacturing company with three production cost centres: forging, stamping and finishing. The following are the expected factory expenses for the forthcoming year:

	£
Rent and rates	14,625
Depreciation of machinery	8,000
Insurance of machinery	680
Supervisory salaries	42,790
Heating and lighting	4,420

Cost centre information is:

	Forging	Stamping	Finishing
Floor area (sq m)	400	600	300
Value of machinery	£30,000	£40,000	£10,000
Number of production-line employees	4	5	2

You are to:

(a) Apportion the expenses to the cost centres, stating the basis of apportionment.

(b) Calculate the overhead absorption rate (to two decimal places) of each cost centre, based on direct labour hours. Note that the company works a 35-hour week for 48 weeks a year.

BUDGETED PRODUCTION OVERHEAD SCHEDULE
for next month

Overhead	Basis of apportionment	Total £	Processing £	Packing £	Quality Assurance £	Stores £	Maintenance £
Rent and rates		4,500					
Supervisory salaries		3,690					
Depreciation of machinery		2,640					
Canteen costs		360					
TOTAL		11,190					

5.4 Wyvern Private Hospital plc has two patient wards – a day care ward for minor operations where the patients go home at the end of the day, and a surgical ward for patients who remain in the hospital for several days. There are two service departments – the operating theatre and administration.

The overheads of each department for last month were as follows:

		£
•	day care ward	28,750
•	surgical ward	42,110
•	operating theatre	32,260
•	administration	9,075

The basis for re-apportioning the overheads of the service departments is:

• operating theatre, on the number of operations carried out – day care ward, 160; surgical ward, 120

• administration, on the number of staff in each department – day care ward, 10; surgical ward, 25; operating theatre, 20

You are to use the step-down method to re-apportion the two service department overheads to the two patient wards.

5.5 Fox Furniture Limited makes tables and chairs for school and college use. There are two production lines – tables, and chairs – and two service departments – stores and maintenance.

The overheads of each department for last month were as follows:

		£
•	tables	12,000
•	chairs	8,000
•	stores	3,000
•	maintenance	2,000

The basis for re-apportioning the overheads of the service departments is:

• stores, on the number of requisitions – tables, 100; chairs, 80; maintenance, 20

• maintenance, on the value of equipment in each department – tables, £30,000; chairs, £20,000

You are to use the step-down method to re-apportion the two service department overheads to the two production departments.

5.6 Steel Forgings (Rowcester) Limited is a heavy engineering business making parts for the car industry. The factory works a 35-hour week and is divided into three manufacturing divisions, with each making a different type of steel forging. Details of last week's production are as follows:

	Division 1	Division 2	Division 3
Direct materials	£3,260	£4,940	£8,760
Direct labour	£1,810	£2,525	£2,850
Number of production-line employees	5	8	10
Number of machine hours	150	250	300
Number of units produced	2,000	2,500	1,000

Production overheads were £10,000 for last week.

You are to:

(a) suggest two different methods by which overheads can be absorbed, and calculate the appropriate overhead absorption rates

(b) calculate the production cost per unit of output in each division using the two different methods of overhead absorption

(c) compare the results of your calculations and suggest the most appropriate method of overhead absorption for this business

Note: where appropriate, round answers to the nearest penny

5.7 Jean-E-Us Limited manufactures denim jeans that are sold to various clothing retailers. The company's operations are organised by departments, as follows:
- Warehouse
- Manufacturing
- Sales
- Accounting

The budgeted and actual fixed overheads of the company for the four weeks ended 27 October 2007 were as follows:

	£
Depreciation of fixed assets	5,000
Rent	6,000
Other property overheads	4,000
Accounting overheads	2,500
Staff costs:	
– warehouse	4,600
– indirect manufacturing	10,500
– sales	7,340
– accounting	3,250
Total budgeted and actual fixed overheads	43,190

The following information is also relevant:

Department	% of floor space occupied	Net book value of fixed assets £000
Warehouse	30%	100
Manufacturing	40%	300
Sales	20%	50
Accounting	10%	50
	100%	500

Overheads are allocated and apportioned between departments using the most appropriate basis.

Task 1

Please see next page.

Task 2

Manufacturing fixed overheads are absorbed on the basis of budgeted machine hours. The budgeted number of machine hours for the four weeks ended 27 October 2007 was 2,000 hours.

You are to calculate the budgeted fixed overhead absorption rate for the manufacturing department for the period.

5.8 Milestone Motors Limited sells and services cars. The company's operations are organised into three profit centres and one cost centre, as follows:

Profit centres
- New car sales
- Used car sales
- Servicing

Cost centre
- Administration

The budgeted and actual fixed overheads of the company for the four weeks ended 28 April 2007 were as follows:

	£
Depreciation of fixed assets	8,400
Rent	10,000
Other property overheads	4,500
Staff costs:	
– new car sales	11,080
– used car sales	7,390
– servicing	9,975
– administration	6,850
Administration overheads	3,860
Total budgeted and actual fixed overheads	62,055

continued on page 40

Activity 5.7: Task 1

Complete the following table showing:

- the basis for allocation or apportionment of each overhead
- the allocation and apportionment of fixed overheads between the four departments

Fixed overheads for four weeks ended 27 October 2007	Basis	Total £	Warehouse £	Manufacturing £	Sales £	Accounting £
Depreciation		5,000				
Rent		6,000				
Other property overheads		4,000				
Accounting overheads		2,500				
Staff costs		25,690				
		43,190				

The following information is also relevant:

Profit/Cost centre	% of floor space occupied	Net book value of fixed assets £000
New car sales	40%	50
Used car sales	30%	30
Servicing	20%	100
Administration	10%	20
	100%	200

Overheads are allocated and apportioned using the most appropriate basis. The total administration overheads are then re-apportioned to the three profit centres using the following percentages.

- New car sales   20%
- Used car sales   30%
- Servicing   50%

Task 1

Please see next page.

Task 2

Servicing centre fixed overheads are absorbed on the basis of budgeted direct labour hours. The budgeted number of direct labour hours for the servicing centre during the four weeks ended 28 April 2007 was 1,025 hours.

You are to calculate the budgeted fixed overhead absorption rate per direct labour hour for the servicing centre during the period.

5.9   Garden Cottage Limited manufactures 'homestyle' soups which are sold through supermarkets and convenience stores. The soups pass through two departments – kitchen and canning. Details of overheads for the departments for the four weeks ended 16 June 2007 are as follows:

Kitchen Department

- overhead absorption rate is £7.00 per direct labour hour
- direct labour hours worked were 800
- actual cost of production overhead was £5,000

Canning Department

- overhead absorption rate is £8.00 per machine hour
- machine hours worked were 400
- actual cost of production overhead was £3,500

continued on page 42

Activity 5.8: Task 1

Complete the following table showing:

- the basis for allocation or apportionment of each overhead;
- the allocation and apportionment of fixed overheads between the four centres;
- the re-apportionment of the total administration overheads.

Fixed overheads for four weeks ended 28 April 2007	Basis	Total £	New Car Sales £	Used Car Sales £	Servicing £	Administration £
Depreciation of fixed assets		8,400				
Rent		10,000				
Other property overheads		4,500				
Staff costs		35,295				
Administration overheads		3,860				
		62,055				( )
Administration		62,055				–

The following cost accounting codes are in use to record overheads:

code number	description
2000	work-in-progress
2100	production overheads: kitchen department
2200	production overheads: canning department
4000	profit and loss account

As an accounts assistant at Garden Cottage Limited, you are asked to prepare the two production overheads accounts below and to fill in the table as at 16 June 2007 to account for the overheads and the over- and under-absorption of overheads.

Dr	Production Overheads Account: Kitchen Department		Cr
2007	£	2007	£

Dr	Production Overheads Account: Canning Department		Cr
2007	£	2007	£

2007	Code	Debit	Credit

6 METHODS OF COSTING

6.1 Wyvern Engineers Limited is a company which specialises in making parts for the car industry. The following Job Cost Sheet has been prepared by you, the Accounting Technician, for the actual costs of manufacture of a batch of gearbox casings for Mawgam Cars, a local specialist builder of touring cars:

JOB NO 471/99			
for gearbox casings			
Customer: Mawgam Cars			

2007		**ACTUAL COSTS £**
	Direct Materials	
8 Sep	MR 3141	422
10 Sep	MR 3152	286
10 Sep	MRN 58	(145)
	Direct Labour	
10 Sep	Wages analysis (30 hours)	420
	Direct Expenses	
8 Sep	Engineer's fee	250
	Production Overheads	345
	TOTAL COST	1,578

Note: Wyvern Engineers uses a labour hour rate for absorbing production overheads.

Your assistant asks you to explain the following about the Job Cost Sheet:

(a)   What does the transaction 'MR 3141' on 8 September mean?

(b)   What does the transaction 'MRN 58' on 10 September mean?

(c)   Where has the information on direct labour hours come from?

(d)   Why is the engineer's fee shown as a direct expense?

(e)   What is the absorption rate for production overheads?

6.2 OB Printers has been asked by John Dun, a local poet, to quote for the cost of printing a small book of poetry. John Dun is not sure how many copies to order, and has asked for quotations for 500, 1,000 and 2,000 copies.

The estimates by OB Printers are as follows:

Setting up the printing machine:	6 hours at £10.00 per hour
Artwork:	7 hours at £12.00 per hour
Typesetting:	20 hours at £15.00 per hour
Paper (for 500 copies):	£100.00
Other printing consumables (for 500 copies):	£50.00
Direct labour (for 500 copies):	5 hours at £13.00 per hour
Production overheads:	80% of direct labour costs
Profit:	25% on cost price

You are to:

(a)   prepare the Job Cost Sheet (see next page) for 500, 1,000 and 2,000 copies, and also show the selling prices

(b)   calculate the cost per book (to the nearest penny) to the author at each of the three different production levels

(c)   respond to John Dun who, on seeing the quotations, says:

"Why is the price per copy so high for 500 copies? I am a starving poet, and I can't afford to have a large quantity printed. If the book sells well I shall regret not having had 2,000 copies printed."

JOB NO 12345

Poetry book for John Dun

	NUMBER OF COPIES		
	500	1,000	2,000
	£	£	£
Fixed Costs			
Setting up machine			
Artwork			
Typesetting			
Direct Materials			
Paper			
Other printing consumables			
Direct Labour			
Production Overheads			
TOTAL COST			
Profit (25% of total cost)			
SELLING PRICE			

6.3   A manufacturer of security alarms has the following information concerning the first month of production:

	£
direct materials	10,725
direct labour	6,600
production overheads	3,900
security alarms completed	2,750
security alarms in progress	500

The work-in-progress is complete as regards materials, but is 50% complete as regards direct labour and production overheads.

You are to:

(a)   complete the schedule below in order to calculate the cost per security alarm for the first month's production

(b)   calculate the month-end valuation for work-in-progress

Note: use the average cost basis for your calculations

Cost element	Costs	Completed Units	Work-in-progress			Total Equivalent Units	Cost per Unit	WIP valuation
			Units	% complete	Equivalent Units			
	A	B	C	D	E	F	G	H
					C x D	B + E	A ÷ F	E x G
	£						£	£
Direct materials								
Direct labour								
Production overheads								
Total								

6.4 Rowcester Limited makes 'older style' radios. At the beginning of January, following demand from shops over the Christmas period, there is no opening work-in-progress.

. The costs of production during January were as follows:

	£
direct materials	98,500
direct labour	43,645
production overheads	50,525

At the end of January, 18,000 radios had been completed, and 7,000 radios remained in progress. The closing work-in-progress was complete as regards direct materials, and 50% complete as regards direct labour and overheads.

You are to complete the schedule below in order to:

(a) calculate the cost per radio for completed output in January

(b) calculate the value of work-in-progress at the end of January

Note: use the average cost basis for your calculations

Cost element	Costs	Completed Units	Work-in-progress			Total Equivalent Units	Cost per Unit	WIP valuation
			Units	% complete	Equivalent Units			
	A	B	C	D	E	F	G	H
					$C \times D$	$B + E$	$A \div F$	$E \times G$
	£						£	£
Direct materials								
Direct labour								
Production overheads								
Total								

6.5 Wyvern Chemicals Limited produces a chemical, which is made in one production process.

For the four weeks ended 9 April 2007, the company input 65,000 litres of direct materials, had an output of 60,000 litres and a normal loss of 5,000 litres. The input costs were: materials £19,500, labour £13,000, overheads £9,750. Normal losses were sold to a specialist reprocessing company for 5p per litre.

There was no opening or closing stock at the beginning and end of the process; all output was complete.

As an accounts assistant, you are to prepare the process account and the normal loss account for the four weeks ended 9 April 2007.

6.6 Hawke Limited produces a washing powder called 'CleanO', which is made in one production process.

For the four weeks ended 24 September 2007, the company input 84,000 kilos of direct materials, had an output of 81,000 kilos – the difference of 3,000 kilos was made up of a normal loss of 4,000 kilos and an abnormal gain of 1,000 kilos.

The input costs were: materials £16,800, labour £12,600, overheads £4,200. All losses were sold to a specialist reprocessing company for 20p per kilo.

There was no opening or closing stock at the beginning and end of the process; all output was complete.

As an accounts assistant, you are to prepare the process account, the abnormal gain account, and the normal loss account for the four weeks ended 24 September 2007.

6.7 Burncoose Limited is a manufacturer of vitamin tablets. Its best-selling product, called 'Vita', is made in two production processes before completion and transfer to finished goods stock.

For the four weeks ended 16 July 2007, details of production of 'Vita' were as follows:

	Process 1	Process 2
Direct materials (5,000 kilos)	£2,000	–
Labour	£1,000	£1,125
Overhead	£500	£675
Normal loss in process of input	5%	3%
Output	4,500 kilos	4,400 kilos
Scrap value of all losses	£0.20 per kilo	£0.40 per kilo

There was no opening or closing stock at the beginning and end of either process; all output was complete. All losses were sold to a specialist reprocessing company.

As an accounts assistant, you are to prepare the following accounts for the four weeks ended 16 July 2007:

• process 1 account

• process 2 account

• normal loss account

• abnormal loss account

• abnormal gain account

Note: calculate costs per unit of expected output to the nearest penny.

7 BOOK-KEEPING FOR COSTING

7.1 In a manufacturing account, indirect materials and indirect labour form part of:

(a)   prime cost

(b)   production overheads

(c)   non-production overheads

(d)   indirect expenses

Answer (a) or (b) or (c) or (d)

7.2 Allocate the following costs (tick the appropriate column):

	manufacturing account	profit and loss account
(a) salaries of sales staff		
(b) wages of production-line employees		
(c) royalty paid to designer of product		
(d) straight-line depreciation of factory machinery		
(e) factory power costs		
(f) re-decoration of administration offices		
(g) units of service depreciation of photocopier in administration office		
(h) bank overdraft interest		
(i) overtime paid to production-line employees		

7.3 The following figures relate to the accounts of Middleton Manufacturing Limited for the year ended 31 December 2007:

	£
Stocks at 1 January 2007:	
Raw materials	25,250
Finished goods	12,380
Stocks at 31 December 2007:	
Raw materials	29,610
Finished goods	11,490
Expenditure during year:	
Purchases of raw materials	75,340
Factory wages – direct	54,690
Factory wages – indirect	22,330
Factory rent and rates	7,380
Factory power	4,250
Depreciation of factory machinery	2,500
Factory maintenance	1,870
Sundry factory expenses	1,140
Non-production overheads	46,730
Sales of finished goods	286,940

Note: Factory power is to be treated as a production overhead.

You are to prepare the year-end:

• manufacturing account

• profit and loss account

Note: please see the Appendix at the end of the book for specimen formats of a manufacturing account and a profit and loss account.

7.4 The following figures relate to the accounts of Ryedale Limited, a manufacturing business, for the year ended 31 October 2007:

	£
Stocks of raw materials at 1 November 2006	41,210
Stocks of raw materials, 31 October 2007	46,380
Stocks of finished goods, 1 November 2006	29,470
Stocks of finished goods, 31 October 2007	38,290
Purchases of raw materials	311,050
Sales of finished goods	874,360
Rent and rates	35,640
Factory wages – direct	180,860
Factory wages – indirect	45,170
Factory power	12,040
Factory heat and light	5,030
Factory sundry expenses and maintenance	10,390
Administration salaries	154,610
Advertising	30,780
Office expenses	10,390
Depreciation of factory plant and machinery	12,500
Depreciation of office equipment	2,500

Additional information:
- factory power is to be treated as a production overhead
- rent and rates are to be allocated 75% to manufacturing and 25% to administration

You are to prepare the year-end:
- manufacturing account
- profit and loss account

Note: please see the Appendix (page 146) for specimen formats of a manufacturing account and a profit and loss account.

7.5 Shah and Company is a manufacturing business which uses an integrated book-keeping system for its costing and financial accounting.

At 1 January 2007, the first day of a new financial year, the company has a number of balances in its ledger as shown on the next few pages.

During January the following transactions took place:

	£
Direct materials bought on credit	12,500
Direct labour costs paid by cheque	10,500
Production overheads paid by cheque	4,000
Non-production overheads paid by cheque	5,000
Credit sales	38,000
Receipts from debtors	41,000
Paid to creditors	12,000
Direct materials transferred to work-in-progress	13,000
Work-in-progress transferred to finished goods	28,000
Finished goods transferred to cost of sales	27,000

You are to:

(a) Record the above transactions in the integrated book-keeping system of Shah and Company, using the accounts on the next four pages, and show the net profit for the month. (Note that the full cost of direct labour and production overheads is to be transferred to work-in-progress.)

(b) Show the trial balance at 31 January 2007, after preparing the profit and loss account in the double-entry accounts.

Dr		**Capital Account**		Cr
2007		£	2007	£
			1 Jan Balance b/d	40,000

Dr		**Machinery Account**		Cr
2007		£	2007	£
1 Jan Balance b/d		15,000		

Dr		**Office Equipment Account**		Cr
2007		£	2007	£
1 Jan Balance b/d		8,000		

Dr		**Bank Account**		Cr
2007		£	2007	£
1 Jan Balance b/d		5,500		

Dr		**Materials Account**			Cr
2007		£	2007		£
1 Jan	Balance b/d	3,500			

Dr		**Work-in-Progress Account**			Cr
2007		£	2007		£
1 Jan	Balance b/d	3,000			

Dr		**Finished Goods Account**			Cr
2007		£	2007		£
1 Jan	Balance b/d	4,000			

Dr		**Debtors' Account**			Cr
2007		£	2007		£
1 Jan	Balance b/d	5,000			

Dr	**Creditors' Account**		Cr
2007	£	2007	£
		1 Jan Balance b/d	4,000

Dr	**Labour Costs Account**		Cr
2007	£	2007	£

Dr	**Production Overheads Account**		Cr
2007	£	2007	£

Dr	**Non-Production Overheads Account**		Cr
2007	£	2007	£

Dr		Sales Account		Cr
2007	£	2007		£

Dr		Cost of Sales Account		Cr
2007	£	2007		£

Dr		Profit and Loss Account		Cr
2007	£	2007		£

7.6 Albion Limited, a manufacturing company, has three departments – moulding, assembly and finishing. The company uses a budgeted overhead absorption rate based on direct labour hours.

The following data relates to production week 46:

	Moulding Department	Assembly Department	Finishing Department
Actual overheads incurred	£1,246	£2,021	£912
Budgeted absorption rate per direct labour hour	£10.40	£12.80	£9.50
Actual direct labour hours worked	125	155	96
Overhead absorbed			
(Under-)/over-absorption of overheads			

You are to complete for each department:

(a) the table (above) to show the amount of overhead absorbed and the under- or over-absorption of overheads

(b) the production overheads accounts (below), including any transfer to profit and loss account

Dr   **Production Overheads Account: Moulding Department**   Cr

	£		£
Bank (overheads incurred)	1,246		

Dr   **Production Overheads Account: Assembly Department**   Cr

	£		£
Bank (overheads incurred)	2,021		

Dr   **Production Overheads Account: Finishing Department**   Cr

	£		£
Bank (overheads incurred)	912		

(c) What effect will this under- or over-absorption have on budgeted profits?

7.7 The data which follows relates to the finishing department of Bringsty Manufacturing. In this department overheads are recovered on the basis of machine hours.

Finishing Department	Period ending 30 June 2007
Budgeted overhead	£109,931
Budgeted machine hours	10,550
Budgeted overhead absorption rate	
Actual machine hours	10,350
Overhead absorbed	
Actual overhead	£114,592
(Under-)/over-absorption of overhead	

As an accounts assistant you are to:

(a) Complete the table above

(b) Write a memorandum to the Accountant which explains:

– the consequences of the results for the period

– the possible causes

– the effect on the costing of jobs which passed through the finishing department during the period

– possible action to be taken for the future

7.8 Wye (Horticultural) Limited produces a liquid fertiliser for garden flowers called 'GreenGrow', which is made in one production process.

For the four weeks ended 22 October 2007, the company input 22,000 litres of direct materials, and had an output of 20,400 litres – the difference of 1,600 litres was made up of a normal loss of 2,000 litres and an abnormal gain of 400 litres.

The input costs were: materials £11,000, labour £7,700, overheads £5,500. All losses were sold to a specialist reprocessing company for 10p per litre.

There was no opening or closing stock at the beginning and end of the process; all output was complete.

As an accounts assistant, you are to prepare the process account, the abnormal gain account, and the normal loss account for the four weeks ended 22 October 2007.

7.9 Goonvrea Limited manufactures a chemical, 'Maravose', within two separate processes. For the week-ended 17 September 2007 the details were:

- *Process 1*

    - materials input, 4,000 kilos at £5 per kilo

    - labour, £4,360

    - overheads, £2,960

- *Process 2*

    - materials input, 3,500 kilos at £4 per kilo

    - labour, £2,640

    - overheads, £1,790

Normal outputs are:

- Process 1, 95% of input

- Process 2, 90% of input

All losses are sold at a scrap value of £0.75 per kilo to a specialist reprocessing company.

There was no work-in-progress at either the beginning or end of the week.

Output during the week was 3,700 kilos from Process 1 and 6,600 kilos from Process 2.

As an accounts assistant at Goonvrea Limited you are asked to prepare the process 1 account, process 2 account, normal loss account, abnormal loss account, and the abnormal gain account for the week ended 17 September 2007. Note: calculate costs per unit of expected output to the nearest penny.

8 SHORT-TERM DECISIONS

8.1 Bert Peters is the owner of a petrol filling station which has the following weekly costs:

Cost of petrol from oil company	80p per litre
Selling price	85p per litre
Fixed overheads	£750

You are to:

• Prepare a table showing costs, sales revenue, and profit or loss for sale of petrol in multiples of 1,000 litres up to 20,000 litres.

• If sales are currently 18,000 litres each week, what is the margin of safety, expressed as a percentage and in litres?

8.2 Kings B & B is a bed and breakfast establishment that caters for individual travellers who want a good night's sleep in a clean bed with a hearty breakfast. There are 10 single bedrooms available, and bed and breakfast is priced at £22 per person per night. Kings B & B is open 7 nights a week.

The following are typical costs:

	weekly costs (for the whole place) £	costs per guest night £
Heating and lighting	42	
Breakfast food		4
Cleaning staff – basic pay	100	
Cleaning staff – bonus		2
Administration	90	
Laundry		3
Breakfast staff	72	
Other overheads	60	

You are to:

(a) Calculate the fixed costs per week and the contribution per guest per night.

(b) Calculate the number of guests per night it would take to break-even.

(c) Calculate the weekly profit or loss if there were 42 guest nights in a week (ie an average of 6 guests on each of the 7 nights).

8.3   Peter Parkinson is a central heating engineer who has designed a special type of thermostatic valve for use in heating systems. He has decided to set up in business to manufacture the product and he has carried out market research which suggests that demand for the product will be between 9,000 units and 20,000 units each year. Accordingly he has produced the following forecasts at different levels of production and sales:

sales (number of units)	9,000	12,000	15,000	20,000
direct materials	£27,000	£36,000	£45,000	£60,000
direct labour	£9,000	£12,000	£15,000	£20,000
production overheads	£66,000	£72,000	£78,000	£88,000

Each thermostatic valve will sell for £10.

Peter asks you to help him interpret the results, and in particular he wishes to know:

(a)   the profit or loss he will make at each level of production

(b)   the break-even point

(c)   the fixed amount of production overheads

One market research survey suggested that a sales level of 30,000 units each year might be achieved. In the form of a report, you, as an accounts assistant, are to:

•   rework the forecast at this sales level and calculate the net profit or loss which will be achieved

•   advise Peter Parkinson of any limitations and the usefulness of your figures at this level of production

8.4   Wyvern Porcelain Limited produces decorated porcelain figures which are sold in quality shops both in the UK and abroad. The figures are especially popular with holidaymakers from other countries who visit the factory and see the figures being made.

There are three ranges of porcelain figures – 'people', 'animals' and 'birds'. The expected monthly costs and sales information for each range is as follows:

Product	'People'	'Animals'	'Birds'
Sales and production units*	1,000	2,000	2,700
Labour hours per month	1,500	1,000	900
Total sales revenue	£60,000	£55,000	£47,250
Total direct materials	£5,000	£6,000	£5,400
Total direct labour	£15,000	£10,000	£9,000
Total variable overheads	£10,000	£9,000	£8,000

* note: a unit is a porcelain figure

The total expected monthly fixed costs relating to the production of all porcelain figures are £45,400.

As an accounts assistant at Wyvern Porcelain Limited, you are to carry out the following tasks.

Task 1

Complete the table below to show for each product range the expected contribution per unit.

Product	'People' £	'Animals' £	'Birds' £
Selling price per unit			
Less: Unit variable costs			
Direct materials			
Direct labour			
Variable overheads			
Contribution per unit			

Task 2

If the company only produces the 'People' range, calculate the number of units it would need to make and sell each month to cover the fixed costs of £45,400.

Task 3

Making and painting the porcelain figures are highly skilled tasks, and unskilled labour cannot be brought in to cover for absent staff.

Unfortunately, because of staff illness, the available labour hours are reduced from 3,400 to 2,800. The finance director asks you to calculate the contribution of each unit (porcelain figure) per labour hour.

Using the data from Task 1, complete the table below.

Product	'People'	'Animals'	'Birds'
Contribution per unit			
Labour hours per unit			
Contribution per labour hour			

Task 4

Using the data from Task 3, calculate how many units of each of product ranges 'People', 'Animals' and 'Birds' the company should make and sell in order to maximise its profits using 2,800 labour hours.

8.5   Mercia Airways is a local airline which flies to short-haul destinations within the UK and Europe. The costs of weekly flight MA 005 to Rome, which uses a 100 seater aircraft are as follows:

direct materials	£12.50 per passenger
direct labour	£10.00 per passenger
direct expenses	£2.50 per passenger
fixed overheads	£3,500 per flight

For next week's flight, sixty seats have been sold at a standard-class fare of £100 each.

You are to calculate:

*   the absorption cost per seat on this flight with sixty seats sold
*   the marginal cost per seat
*   the profit or loss if no further tickets are sold for this flight

The Marketing Manager thinks it unlikely that any further standard-class fares will be sold. There are two possibilities that she must consider:

*   to release the surplus seats to a firm that sells cheap flights: the airline will receive £45 for each seat sold and, from past experience, the marketing manager expects thirty seats to be sold
*   to sell all forty spare seats to a local newspaper, which will offer them as prizes for a 'spot-the-ball' competition: the newspaper will pay £35 per seat

As an accounts assistant, you are to write a memorandum to the Marketing Manager, advising whether either of these possibilities should be considered; explain your reasoning, and illustrate your answer with profit statements.

8.6   The Last Company is famous for its 'Snowdon' range of hill-walking boots. The management of the company is considering the production for next year and has asked for help with certain financial decisions.

The following information is available:

wholesale selling price (per pair)	£60
direct materials (per pair)	£20
direct labour (per pair)	£18
fixed overheads	£200,000 per year

The company is planning to manufacture 12,500 pairs of boots next year.

You are to calculate:

*   the absorption cost per pair
*   the marginal cost per pair
*   the profit or loss if 12,500 pairs of boots are sold

A mail order company, Sales-by-Post Limited, has approached The Last Company with a view to selling the 'Snowdon' boot through its catalogue. Sales-by-Post offers two contracts:

- either 2,500 pairs of boots at £45 per pair

- or 5,000 pairs of boots at £37 per pair

As The Last Company usually sells through specialist shops, it is not expected that 'normal' sales will be affected. These 'special orders' are within the capacity of the factory, and fixed overheads will remain unchanged.

As an accounts assistant, you are to write a memorandum to the Managing Director advising her whether these offers should be accepted; illustrate your answer with profit statements.

8.7 Tempus Limited makes reproduction antique clocks. The company produces 2,500 clocks each year and the costs per unit of output are:

	£
direct materials	20.50
direct labour	31.00
variable production overheads	5.50
fixed production overheads	4.00
fixed non-production overheads	3.00
	64.00

The selling price of each clock is £80.00

The Managing Director of the business, Jane Haslam, has been thinking about how to increase profits for next year. She has asked you, as an accounts assistant, to look at the following two proposals from a cost accounting viewpoint.

Proposal 1

To reduce the selling price of each clock to £70.00. This is expected to increase sales by 1,000 clocks each year to a total of 3,500 clocks. Apart from changes in variable costs, there would be no change in fixed costs.

Proposal 2

To increase the selling price of each clock to £100.00. This is expected to reduce sales by 500 clocks each year to a total of 2,000 clocks. Apart from changes in variable costs, there would be a reduction of £3,000 in fixed production overheads.

You are to write a memorandum to Jane Haslam, the Managing Director, stating your advice, giving reasons and workings. Each of the two proposals is to be considered on its own merits without reference to the other proposal.

8.8 Durning Limited manufactures one product, the Durn. For the month of April 2007 the following information is available:

number of units manufactured	10,000
number of units sold	8,000
selling price	£4 per unit
direct materials for month	£8,000
direct labour for month	£16,000
fixed production overheads for month	£10,000

There was no finished goods stock at the start of the month. Both direct materials and direct labour behave as variable costs.

You are to:

(a) produce profit statements for April 2007, using:

- marginal costing
- absorption costing

(b) explain briefly the reason for the difference between recorded profits under the alternative costing systems

9 LONG-TERM DECISIONS

TABLE OF DISCOUNTED CASH FLOW FACTORS								
Cost of capital/ rate of return	10%	12%	14%	16%	18%	20%	22%	24%
Year 1	0.909	0.893	0.877	0.862	0.847	0.833	0.820	0.806
Year 2	0.826	0.797	0.769	0.743	0.718	0.694	0.672	0.650
Year 3	0.751	0.712	0.675	0.641	0.609	0.579	0.551	0.524
Year 4	0.683	0.636	0.592	0.552	0.516	0.482	0.451	0.423
Year 5	0.621	0.567	0.519	0.476	0.437	0.402	0.370	0.341
Year 6	0.564	0.507	0.456	0.410	0.370	0.335	0.303	0.275

Tutorial note: In Examinations you will always be given the appropriate factors.

9.1 The following information relates to two major capital investment projects being considered by Newell Limited. For financial reasons, only one project can be accepted.

	Project Ess	Project Tee
	£	£
Initial cost at the beginning of the project	100,000	115,000
Net cash inflows, year: 1	40,000	50,000
2	60,000	35,000
3	20,000	30,000
4	20,000	30,000
5	10,000	30,000
Expected scrap value at end of year 5	5,000	7,500

The initial cost occurs at the beginning of the project and you may assume that the net cash inflows will arise at the end of each year. Newell Limited requires an annual rate of return of 10 per cent.

To help the Managing Director of Newell Limited make her decision, as accounts assistant you are to:

- produce numerical assessments of the two projects based on the following capital investment appraisal methods:
  - (a)   the payback period
  - (b)   the net present value

- write a report to the Managing Director on the relative merits of the project appraisal methods, and advise her which capital investment, if either, should be undertaken

9.2 A capital investment project has the following expected cash flows over its life of three years:

	£
Initial cost at the beginning of the project	(55,000)
Net cash inflows, year: 1	19,376
2	28,491
3	21,053

The expected scrap value at the end of year 3 is nil.

You are to:

(a) Calculate the net present value of the project at annual rates of return of 10 per cent, 12 per cent and 14 per cent. Calculate all money amounts to the nearest £.

(b) What do your calculations in part (a) tell you about this project?

9.3 You work as an accounts assistant for the Chester Carpet Company, which makes quality carpets. Currently you are working on the appraisal of a capital investment project to purchase a new machine for the production department in December 2007.

The machine will cost £65,000 and will have a useful life of four years. The cash inflows are expected to be:

	£
2008	17,000
2009	25,000
2010	31,000
2011	24,000

At the end of the project, the machine will be sold as scrap for an expected amount of £4,000.

Chester Carpet Company requires an annual rate of return of 10 per cent for net present value, and a maximum payback period of three years.

Task 1

Use the working paper on the next page to calculate the net present value and the payback period of the proposed project. Ignore inflation and calculate all money amounts to the nearest £.

Task 2

Write a report, dated 24 November 2007, to the General Manager evaluating the proposal from a financial viewpoint. State any assumptions you have made in your analysis.

CHESTER CARPET LIMITED
Working paper for the financial appraisal of a new machine
for the production department

DISCOUNTED CASH FLOW

Year	Cash Flow	Discount Factor at 10%	Discounted Cash Flow
	£		£
2007	_____	1.000	_____
2008	_____	0.909	_____
2009	_____	0.826	_____
2010	_____	0.751	_____
2011	_____	0.683	_____
Net Present Value (NPV)			_____

PAYBACK PERIOD

Year	Cash Flow	Cumulative Cash Flow
	£	£
2007	_____	_____
2008	_____	_____
2009	_____	_____
2010	_____	_____
2011	_____	_____

Payback period = _____

9.4 Towan Kitchens Limited makes 'flat-pack' kitchens which are sold to the public in DIY stores. You are an accounts assistant and have just received the following memorandum from the General Manager:

MEMORANDUM

To: Accounts Assistant

From: General Manager

Date: 15 September 2007

Manufacture of kitchen worktops

As you know, the manufacture of worktops is currently contracted out to another company at a cost to us of £200,000 per year. The production manager has proposed that we should buy the special equipment needed to do the work ourselves in-house, thus making savings on the costs of the contract work. The equipment will cost £300,000 and we will also have to pay the following costs over the next five years:

	operators' wages £	repairs and maintenance £	other costs £
2008	42,000	8,000	33,000
2009	64,000	12,000	37,000
2010	68,000	22,000	42,000
2011	68,000	25,000	44,000
2012	70,000	30,000	45,000

If we go ahead, the equipment will be bought at the end of this year ready for production to start in 2008. At the end of 2012 the equipment will have a scrap value of £10,000.

Please appraise this proposal from a financial viewpoint. I need to know the payback period and the net present value. As you know, the maximum required payback period is three years and, for net present value, we require a return of 14%.

Task 1

Use the working paper on the next page to calculate the net present value and the payback period of the proposed investment. Ignore inflation and calculate all money amounts to the nearest £.

Task 2

Write a report, dated 18 September 2007, to the General Manager evaluating the proposal from a financial viewpoint. State any assumptions you have made in your analysis.

TOWAN KITCHENS LIMITED

Working paper for the financial appraisal of in-house worktop manufacture

CASH FLOWS

Year	Savings £	Total Costs £	Cash Flow £
2007	–	_____	_____
2008	_____	_____	_____
2009	_____	_____	_____
2010	_____	_____	_____
2011	_____	_____	_____
2012	_____	_____	_____

DISCOUNTED CASH FLOW

Year	Cash Flow £	Discount Factor at 14%	Discounted Cash Flow £
2007	_____	1.000	_____
2008	_____	0.877	_____
2009	_____	0.769	_____
2010	_____	0.675	_____
2011	_____	0.592	_____
2012	_____	0.519	_____

Net Present Value (NPV)

PAYBACK PERIOD

Year	Cash Flow £	Cumulative Cash Flow £
2007	_____	_____
2008	_____	_____
2009	_____	_____
2010	_____	_____
2011	_____	_____
2012	_____	_____

Payback period = _____

9.5 The research department of Zelah Chemical Company has discovered a wonder drug which cures the symptoms of the common cold within a matter of hours. The company has decided to develop the new drug – to be called 'Zelahcold' – and the Managing Director has asked you, the accounts assistant, to appraise the financial effects of this project.

For all new projects the company requires an annual rate of return of 10 per cent for net present value, and a maximum payback period of three years in terms of revenue.

You are given the following information relating to this project.

	Year 0 £000	Year 1 £000	Year 2 £000	Year 3 £000	Year 4 £000	Year 5 £000
Development costs	–	110	–	–	–	–
Sales revenue	–	–	55	90	120	120
Variable costs	–	–	30	30	40	35
10% Present value factor	1.000	0.909	0.826	0.751	0.683	0.621

Task 1

Calculate for the new project:

(a)   the payback period

(b)   the net present value

Task 2

Use the data from Task 1 to prepare a report to the Managing Director on the new product. Your report should:

(a)   identify *two* additional items of information relevant to appraising this project

(b)   make a recommendation to accept or reject the project

Practice Examination 1
Twistweave Limited

Element coverage

6.1 record and analyse information relating to direct costs and revenues

6.2 record and analyse information relating to the allocation, apportionment and absorption of overhead costs

6.3 prepare and evaluate estimates of costs and revenues

Suggested time allocation

Three hours and fifteen minutes (to include a recommended fifteen minutes reading time).

PRACTICE EXAMINATION 1
TWISTWEAVE LIMITED

This examination is in TWO sections.

You have to show competence in BOTH sections.

You should therefore attempt and aim to complete EVERY task in BOTH sections.

Blank space for workings is available on the pages, but all essential workings should be included within your answers, where appropriate.

You should spend about 90 minutes on each section.

Both sections are based on Twistweave Ltd.

DATA

Twistweave Ltd makes a single type of fabric, TW1, which is sold to other manufacturing companies, where it is used in various products. The output of TW1 is measured in rolls of fabric. The direct material used by Twistweave Ltd is a special type of thread. The company operates an integrated absorption costing system and uses the Last In First Out method of valuation for issues of material from stores.

You work as an accounting assistant at Twistweave Ltd and have been given the following tasks. Additional data is given as required for the tasks.

SECTION 1

You should spend about 90 minutes on this section.

Tasks 1.1 and 1.2 relate to the budget for the next year. Tasks 1.3 to 1.6 relate to the month of March during the year to which the budget applies.

ADDITIONAL DATA

Twistweave Ltd has the following departments:

> Production
>
> Stores
>
> Administration
>
> Sales

The budgeted fixed overheads for the next year are:

	£
Indirect labour:	
Production	48,000
Stores	36,000
Administration	67,000
Sales	55,000
	206,000
Other administration overheads	45,000
Depreciation	120,000
Premises costs	80,000
Total fixed overheads	451,000

The following information is available:

Department:	Production	Stores	Administration	Sales
Net book value of fixed assets (£000s)	420	100	60	20
Percentage of floor area occupied	60%	20%	10%	10%

Fixed overheads are to be allocated and apportioned between departments using the most appropriate basis.

Task 1.1

Complete the table on the next page showing the allocation and apportionment of fixed overheads between the four departments.

Task 1.1 (continued)

Fixed overheads for the year	Basis	Total £	Production £	Stores £	Administration £	Sales £
Indirect labour		206,000				
Other administration costs		45,000				
Depreciation		120,000				
Premises costs		80,000				
Budgeted fixed overheads		451,000				

ADDITIONAL DATA

Production department fixed overheads are absorbed on the basis of budgeted direct labour hours.

72,000 hours of direct labour are budgeted for the next year.

Task 1.2

Calculate the budgeted fixed overhead absorption rate for the production department for the next year. (You will need to refer to your answer to Task 1.1.)

ADDITIONAL DATA

Tasks 1.3 to 1.6 relate to the month of March during the year to which the budget applies. Production overheads are absorbed in March using the absorption rate calculated in Task 1.2 above.

Task 1.3

Twistweave Ltd uses the LIFO method for valuing issues of material to production and stocks of materials. Complete the stock card for thread shown on the next page. Use the boxes below the card to show your figures for stock issues if there is not room on the stock card itself.

STOCK CARD

Product: Thread (direct material)

Date	Receipts			Issues			Stock		
	Quantity	Unit price £	Total cost £	Quantity	Unit price £	Total £	Quantity	Unit price £	Total £
1 Mar							1,900	50	95,000
5 Mar	500	52	26,000				500	52	26,000
10 Mar				800					
12 Mar	1,000	52	52,000						
17 Mar				800					
19 Mar				300					
23 Mar	1,000	53	53,000						
24 Mar				1,100					
31 Mar c/d									

issue 10 Mar

issue 17 Mar

issue 19 Mar

issue 24 Mar

ADDITIONAL DATA

The following data relates to the direct labour for production of fabric TW1 for the month of March:

Direct labour hours worked =   7,200 hours

Normal time hours   =   6,000 hours

Overtime hours   =   1,200 hours

Normal time rate per hour   =   £6.60

Overtime premium*   =   £3.30

*Total overtime premium is treated as an indirect cost.

Task 1.4

(a)   Complete the table below to record the book-keeping entries for direct wages and overtime premium for the month of March:

	Dr	Cr
Work in progress control account		
Production overhead control account		
Wages control account		

(b)   Referring to your answer to task 1.2, calculate the production overhead absorbed in the month of March.

Task 1.5

Refer to your answer to Task 1.3 to obtain the total value of direct material used in March. (There were no further issues of direct material in March.)

Referring also to your answers to Task 1.4, complete the table below to show:

(a)   the total cost of production of fabric TW1 in March

(b)   the unit cost of production of fabric TW1 in March

Product: TW1 **Month**: March **Output**: 300 rolls	
	£
Direct costs:	
Direct material (thread)	
Direct labour	
Production overheads absorbed	
Total production cost	
Unit cost of production (production cost per roll)	

Task 1.6

Referring to your answer to Task 1.4 (b), show the appropriate entries for production overhead absorbed and for over or under absorption in order to complete and balance the Production Overhead Control Account for March:

Production Overhead Control Account (for March)

Dr   Cr

	£		£
Wages control account	5,000		
Depreciation	7,000		
Premises costs	4,000		

SECTION 2

You should spend about 90 minutes on this section.

ADDITIONAL DATA

The managers of Twistweave Ltd are considering whether to develop a new fabric product, TW2, with different uses from those of TW1. The company would set up a separate department for TW2 and the new product would not affect sales of TW1. The data in this section all relates to the proposal to develop TW2 and is not connected to the tasks in Section 1.

Some forecasts of costs, sales, capital investment and future cash flows have been prepared for the new product.

Budgeted costs have been forecast for the first 6 months of production and sales of TW2, at two different volumes of output, as follows:

Product TW2: Production cost budget for first 6 months		
Output (rolls)	1,000	1,500
	£	£
Direct costs	200,000	300,000
Indirect labour	65,000	90,000
Depreciation	21,000	21,000
Premises costs	13,000	13,000
Total	299,000	424,000

Task 2.1

Identify the fixed, variable and semi-variable costs in the budget for TW2 and separate any semi-variable costs into their fixed and variable parts.

Task 2.2

Using your analysis in Task 2.1, complete the Production cost budget below for a volume of 1,200 rolls of TW2.

Product TW2: Production cost budget for first 6 months	
Output (rolls)	1,200
	£
Direct costs	
Indirect labour	
Depreciation	
Premises costs	
Total	

Task 2.3

Using your answers to Task 2.1, calculate the number of rolls of TW2 to be made and sold in the first 6 months in order to break even, assuming the budgeted selling price is £320 per roll.

Task 2.4

Complete the table below to show the volume of production and sales of TW2 required in order to obtain a profit of £42,000 from this product in the first 6 months:

Total fixed costs	
Required profit	
Total contribution required	
Contribution per unit	
Volume required	

ADDITIONAL DATA

Twistweave Ltd requires a payback period of less than 3 years and a rate of return of 12% per year on new projects. The following forecasts have been prepared, showing the relevant cash flows for TW2 over a five year period.

	Year 1 £000s	Year 2 £000s	Year 3 £000s	Year 4 £000s	Year 5 £000s
Initial investment	(300)				
Sales revenue		600	700	800	700
Relevant costs excluding depreciation		500	570	660	600
12% present value factor	0.893	0.797	0.712	0.636	0.567

Task 2.5

Calculate for the fabric TW2 project:

(a)   the payback period

(b)   the net present value (using the table below for your workings)

	Year 1 £000s	Year 2 £000s	Year 3 £000s	Year 4 £000s	Year 5 £000s
12% present value factor	0.893	0.797	0.712	0.636	0.567

Task 2.6

Referring to your answers to Task 2.5, write a short report on the proposed new fabric TW2 to the managers of Twistweave Ltd. Your report should include:

• a recommendation as to whether to proceed with the project

• brief comments on the disadvantages of each of the methods used

REPORT

To:

From:

Date:

Practice Examination 2
Chem-Pro Limited

Element coverage

6.1 record and analyse information relating to direct costs and revenues

6.2 record and analyse information relating to the allocation, apportionment and absorption of overhead costs

6.3 prepare and evaluate estimates of costs and revenues

Suggested time allocation

Three hours and fifteen minutes (to include a recommended fifteen minutes reading time).

PRACTICE EXAMINATION 2
CHEM-PRO LIMITED

This examination is in TWO sections.

You have to show competence in BOTH sections.

You should therefore attempt and aim to complete EVERY task in BOTH sections.

Blank space for workings is available on these pages, but all essential workings should be included within your answers, where appropriate.

You should spend about 90 minutes on each section.

Both sections are based on Chem-Pro Ltd.

DATA

Chem-Pro Ltd is a manufacturer of chemicals used in the plastics industry. The company uses an integrated absorption costing system.

You work as an Accounts Assistant for Chem-Pro Ltd and are asked to carry out the following tasks.

SECTION 1

You should spend about 90 minutes on this section.

The tasks in this section all relate to the Processing Division of Chem-Pro Ltd for the month of July.

The direct material is a chemical, XR, measured in litres. Process costing is used in the Processing Division. The output of the Processing Division is Chem-Base, which is measured in litres. Further data will be given where required for the tasks.

The direct material XR is issued to the production process on a weighted average valuation basis.

Task 1.1

Complete the stock card on the next page for chemical XR for the month of July, using the weighted average method.

(Due to the breakdown of a processing machine during the last week of July, there were no further issues of XR in July after those shown.)

STOCK CARD

Stock item: Chemical XR (direct material)　　　　　**Unit:**　litre

Date	Receipts			Issues			Stock		
	Quantity	Unit price £	Total cost £	Quantity	Unit price £	Total £	Quantity	Unit price £	Total £
1 July							12,000	3	36,000
7 July				7,000					
10 July	10,000	3.06	30,600						
14 July				7,000					
17 July	10,000	3.06	30,600						
21 July				8,000					
31 July (balance)									

ADDITIONAL DATA

The following data relates to the direct labour employees who work on production of Chem-Base for the month of July:

Normal time hours worked	5,520 hours
Overtime hours worked	400 hours
Total hours of production	5,920 hours
Idle time due to machine breakdown	780 hours
Total labour hours paid for	6,700 hours

The normal time rate for the idle time is to be treated as an indirect cost.

Normal time rate per hour = £7.00

Overtime premium = £3.50. Total overtime premium is treated as an indirect cost.

Task 1.2

Complete the table below for the direct labour employees for the month of July.

	Total cost £	Direct cost £	Indirect cost £
Normal time hours worked			
Overtime hours worked			
Total hours of production			
Idle time (machine breakdown)			
Total labour hours paid for			

ADDITIONAL DATA

The Processing Division of Chem-Pro Ltd has four departments, shown below with available information:

	Net book value of fixed assets	% time of IT services	% requisitions
Production	£200,000	40%	90%
Stores	£40,000	20%	-
IT Services	£8,000	-	-
Administration	£12,000	40%	10%
	£260,000	100%	100%

The monthly budgeted overheads for the Division amount to £46,500, as shown in the table on the next page. Some budgeted overheads have already been allocated and Premises Costs have been apportioned to the four departments.

Task 1.3

Complete the table on the next page using suitable bases for:

• apportionment of Depreciation

• re-apportionment of IT Services overheads

• re-apportionment of Stores overheads

Note: do not re-apportion Administration overheads.

Chem-Pro Ltd: Processing Division Monthly Overhead Budget

	Basis	Total £	Production £	Stores £	IT Services £	Administration £
Allocated overheads	Allocated	29,300	8,860	4,000	9,240	7,200
Premises costs	Floor area	12,000	9,000	1,800	600	600
Depreciation		5,200				
Subtotals						
Reapportion IT Services						
Subtotals						
Re-apportion Stores						
Totals						

ADDITIONAL DATA

The total monthly Budgeted Production Overhead from your answer to Task 1.3 is to be used to calculate the Production Overhead absorption rate, based on budgeted machine hours. The monthly budgeted machine hours are 11,200 hours.

Task 1.4

Calculate the Production Overhead absorption rate.

ADDITIONAL DATA

The actual production overheads in July amounted to £39,000. Due to the machine breakdown, the actual machine hours for the month of July were only 8,510 hours.

Task 1.5

(a)   Using your answer to Task 1.4, calculate the Production Overheads absorbed on the actual 8,510 machine hours and calculate the over or under absorption for the month of July.

(b)   Comment briefly on the reasons why the over or under absorption of Production overhead calculated in (a) above has occurred.

ADDITIONAL DATA

The Processing Division uses process costing in order to determine the cost per litre of the output of Chem-Base. The direct material XR is input to the process. The normal loss is 10% of the material input and this has no scrap value.

Task 1.6

Refer to your answers as follows:

Task 1.1   to determine the total amount in litres and the cost of direct material XR issued to the process during July

Task 1.2   to identify the total direct labour cost for July

Task 1.5   to identify the production overhead absorbed during July

Use these figures and the additional data given above to complete the Process Account for the month of July.

From the completed Process Account, calculate the cost per litre of output of Chem-Base.

Process Account: Chem-Pro Processing for July

Dr					Cr
	Litres	£		Litres	£
Material XR					
Direct labour					
Production overheads absorbed					

Cost per litre of output of Chem-Base =

SECTION 2

You should spend about 90 minutes on this section.

ADDITIONAL DATA

The output of Chem-Base from the Processing Division of Chem-Pro Ltd is sold to the Resins Division of the same company at a price of £8.00 per litre. The Resins Division manufactures three products, P, Q and R. You are given information relating to these products in the table below.

Task 2.1

Complete the three rows that are left blank in the table below.

Product	P	Q	R
Demand per month (units to be made and sold)	3,000	3,000	4,500
Chem-Base per unit (litres)	2.5	2	3
Costs per unit:	£	£	£
Direct material cost (Chem-Base)			
Other variable costs	30	30	30
Total variable costs			
Selling price per unit	100	96	105
Contribution per unit			

Task 2.2

Assuming sufficient resources are available to produce the full demand for each of the products P, Q and R, calculate the total contribution obtained per month in the Resins Division by completing the table below. Refer to your answer to Task 2.1 where required.

Chem-Pro Resins Division Monthly Contribution			
	Demand (units)	Contribution per unit (£)	Total contribution (£)
Product P	3,000		
Product Q	3,000		
Product R	4,500		
Total contribution per month			

ADDITIONAL DATA

The processing machine breakdown in July will result in a shortage of Chem-Base for the Resins Division to use in August. The total Chem-Base available for production of resins P, Q and R will be 19,800 litres for the month.

Task 2.3

Complete the table below to determine the ranking of the three products P, Q and R in terms of their contribution per litre of the material Chem-Base. Refer to your answer to Task 2.1 where required.

Product	P	Q	R
Demand (units)	3,000	3,000	4,500
Chem-Base per unit (litres)	2.5	2	3
Contribution per unit	£	£	£
Contribution per unit per litre of Chem-Base			
Ranking			

Task 2.4

(a)   Complete the table below to determine the production quantities of P, Q, and R that will maximise the Resins Division profit in August, when only 19,800 litres of Chem-Base are available:

Ranking	Product	Units of production and sales	Chem-Base per unit (litres)	Total used (litres)
1				
2				
3				

(b)   Calculate for the Resins Division for August:

- the units of production and sales lost due to the shortage of Chem-Base
- the total contribution lost due to the shortage of Chem-Base

ADDITIONAL DATA

The managers of Chem-Pro Ltd are concerned that machine breakdowns result in financial losses to the company. They are considering upgrading machinery to make it more reliable.

An initial investment (Year 0) of £120,000 would be required. Forecasts of the resulting cash flow (savings) over the following four years are:

	Cash savings
Year 1	£50,000
Year 2	£55,000
Year 3	£60,000
Year 4	£60,000

The residual value of the project at the end of the four years (Year 4) is expected to be £30,000.

A discount rate of 10% is to be used in appraisal of the investment.

Task 2.5

Using the table below for your workings, calculate the payback period and the net present value for the proposed investment in the upgrade of machinery.

Chem-Pro Ltd Proposal to upgrade machinery				
	Cash flow £	Accumulated cash flow £	10% Present value factor	Discounted cash flow £
Year 0			1.000	
Year 1			0.909	
Year 2			0.826	
Year 3			0.751	
Year 4			0.683	
Net Present Value				

Payback period:

Task 2.6

Referring to your answers to Task 2.5, write a short report on the proposed upgrade to the managers of Chem-Pro Ltd. Your report should include:

• a recommendation as to whether to proceed with the project

• one advantage of the upgrade that is not shown in the figures in your analysis

Please see the report format on the next page.

REPORT

To:

From:

Date:

Subject:

Practice Examination 3: Gift Limited

(based on AAT sample material) © AAT, 2003

Element coverage

6.1 record and analyse information relating to direct costs and revenues

6.2 record and analyse information relating to the allocation, apportionment and absorption of overhead costs

6.3 prepare and evaluate estimates of costs and revenues

Suggested time allocation

Three hours and fifteen minutes (to include a recommended fifteen minutes reading time).

PRACTICE EXAMINATION 3
GIFT LIMITED

This examination is in TWO sections.

You have to show competence in BOTH sections.

You should therefore attempt and aim to complete EVERY task in BOTH sections.

Blank space for workings is available on these pages, but all essential workings should be included within your answers, where appropriate.

You should spend about 90 minutes on each section.

Both sections are based on Gift Ltd.

DATA

Gift Ltd manufactures and sells toys. You work as an accounting technician at Gift Ltd, reporting to the Finance Director.

All toys are manufactured using plastic. The biggest selling item is Meg, a toy doll made from pink plastic. The company operates an integrated absorption costing system. Stocks are valued on a first in first out basis.

The Finance Director has given you the tasks that follow in Sections 1 and 2.

SECTION 1

You should spend about 90 minutes on this section.

Task 1.1

Complete the stock card (on the next page) for pink plastic using the FIFO method for valuing issues to production and stocks of materials.

Use the boxes shown below the stock card to show your answers.

STOCK CARD

Product: Pink plastic

Date	Receipts Quantity kgs	Cost per kg £	Total cost £	Issues Quantity kgs	Cost per kg £	Total cost £	Balance Quantity kgs	Total cost £
b/f 1.11.07							10,000	10,000
6.11.07	20,000	1.10	22,000				30,000	32,000
11.11.07				16,000				
17.11.07	10,000	1.20	12,000					
19.11.07				20,000				

issue
11.11.07

issue
19.11.07

ADDITIONAL DATA

All issues of pink plastic are for the manufacture of Meg dolls. The following cost accounting codes are used to record material costs:

Code number	Description
1000	Stock of pink plastic
1100	Work in progress – Meg dolls
3000	Creditors control

Task 1.2

Complete the table below to record separately the two purchases and two issues of pink plastic in the cost accounting records.

Date	Code	Dr	Cr
6 Nov	1000		
6 Nov	3000		
11 Nov	1000		
11 Nov	1100		
17 Nov	1000		
17 Nov	3000		
19 Nov	1000		
19 Nov	1100		

ADDITIONAL DATA

Direct labour overtime payments are included in direct costs. The following data relates to the production of Meg dolls for November:

Total direct labour hours worked	12,000 hours
Normal time hours	10,600 hours
Overtime hours	1,400 hours
Normal time rate per hour	£6 per hour
Overtime premium per hour	£3 per hour

Task 1.3

Calculate the total cost of direct labour for November.

ADDITIONAL DATA

Gift Ltd has the following departments: Warehouse, Manufacturing, Sales, Accounting.

The budgeted and actual fixed overheads of the company for November were as follows:

	£
Depreciation	7,400
Rent	2,500
Other property overheads	3,200
Accounting overheads	6,250
Staff costs:	
Warehouse	4,230
Indirect manufacturing	3,015
Sales	6,520
Accounting	5,160
Total budgeted and actual fixed overheads	38,275

The following information is also relevant:

Department	% of floor space occupied	Net book value of fixed assets £000
Warehouse	15%	180
Manufacturing	70%	540
Sales	10%	-
Accounting	5%	80
	100%	800

Overheads are allocated and apportioned between departments using the most appropriate basis.

Task 1.4

Complete the following table showing the allocation and apportionment of fixed overheads between the four departments.

Fixed overheads for November	Basis	Total £	Warehouse £	Manufacturing £	Sales £	Accounting £
Depreciation		7,400				
Rent		2,500				
Other property overheads		3,200				
Accounting overheads		6,250				
Staff costs		18,925				
		38,275				

ADDITIONAL DATA

Manufacturing fixed overheads are absorbed on the basis of budgeted direct labour hours. The following information relates to the manufacturing department for November:

- The budgeted number of direct labour hours was 20,000 hours.
- The actual direct labour hours worked producing Meg dolls were 12,000 hours.
- 36,000 Meg dolls were produced with a material cost for pink plastic of £39,200.

Task 1.5

Use the data from Task 1.4 to calculate the budgeted fixed overhead absorption rate for the manufacturing department for November.

Task 1.6

Use the information from Tasks 1.3 and 1.5 to complete the table below to show:

(a)   the total cost of production

(b)   the unit cost of production of a Meg doll for November

Product: Meg doll	£
Direct costs	
Pink plastic	
Direct labour	
Indirect costs	
Manufacturing department overheads	
Total cost of production	
Number of Meg dolls produced	
Unit cost of production (to the nearest penny)	

SECTION 2

You should spend about 90 minutes on this section.

DATA

In addition to producing Meg dolls, the company manufactures and sells three types of doll house, products E, C and R. The expected monthly costs and sales information for each product is as follows:

Product	E	C	R
Sales and production units	2,000	1,500	500
Machine hours per month	200	225	175
Total sales revenue	£60,000	£60,000	£30,000
Total direct materials	£20,000	£16,500	£6,000
Total direct labour	£32,000	£24,000	£10,000
Total variable overheads	£4,000	£2,625	£3,500

The total expected monthly fixed costs relating to the production of all doll houses are £4,800.

Task 2.1

Complete the table below to show for each product the expected contribution per unit.

Product	E £	C £	R £
Selling price per unit			
Less: Unit variable costs			
Direct materials			
Direct labour			
Variable overheads			
Contribution per unit			

Task 2.2

If the company only manufactures product E, calculate the number of units it would need to make and sell each month to cover the fixed costs of £4,800.

ADDITIONAL DATA

The breakdown of a machine used in the manufacture of doll houses has reduced available machine time from 600 to 365 hours. The Finance Director asks you to calculate the contribution of each doll house per machine hour.

Task 2.3

Use the data from Task 2.1 to complete the table below.

Product	E £	C £	R £
Contribution per unit			
Machine hours per unit			
Contribution per machine hour			

Task 2.4

Use the data from Task 2.3 to calculate how many units of products E, C and R the company should make and sell to maximize its profits using 365 machine hours.

ADDITIONAL DATA

The company requires an annual rate of return of 10% on any new project. The Managing Director has asked you to appraise the financial effects of introducing a new doll house. You are given the following information relating to this product:

	Year 1 £000	Year 2 £000	Year 3 £000	Year 4 £000	Year 5 £000
Design costs	80				
Sales revenues		30	50	160	50
Variable costs		15	25	80	25
10% Present value factor	0.909	0.826	0.751	0.683	0.621

Task 2.5

Calculate for the new doll house project:

(a)   the payback period

(b)   the net present value

Task 2.6

Use the data from Task 2.5 to prepare a report to the Managing Director on the new doll house project. Your report should:

     (a)   identify TWO additional items of information relevant to appraising this project

     (b)   recommend whether to accept or reject the project based on its net present value

REPORT

To:

From:

Date:

Practice Examination 4
Western Foods Limited

Element coverage

6.1   record and analyse information relating to direct costs and revenues

6.2   record and analyse information relating to the allocation, apportionment and absorption of overhead costs

6.3   prepare and evaluate estimates of costs and revenues

Suggested time allocation

Three hours plus 15 minutes' reading time.

PRACTICE EXAMINATION 4
WESTERN FOODS LIMITED

This examination is in TWO sections.

You have to show competence in BOTH sections.

You should, therefore, attempt and aim to complete EVERY task in BOTH sections.

Blank space for workings is available on these pages, but all essential workings should be included within your answers, where appropriate.

You should spend about 80 minutes on Section 1 and about 100 minutes on Section 2.

Both sections are based on Western Foods Ltd.

DATA

You work as an accounting technician at Western Foods Ltd, a company that manufactures and sells a wide range of food products. Its customers are mainly supermarkets and food wholesalers.

The Management Accountant has given you the following tasks.

SECTION 1

You should spend about 80 minutes on this section.

Task 1.1

Complete the stock record card shown below for raw material J for the month of May 2007. The company uses the First In, First Out (FIFO) method of stock valuation.

Use the boxes shown below the stock card to show your answers.

	Receipts			Issues			Balance	
Date 2007	Quantity kg	Cost per kg £	Total cost £	Quantity kg	Cost per kg £	Total cost £	Quantity kg	Total cost £
Balance as at 1 May							1,500	3,750
12 May	1,000	2.50	2,500				2,500	6,250
17 May				1,000				
24 May	3,000	2.60	7,800					
28 May				2,000				

STOCK RECORD CARD FOR RAW MATERIAL J

ADDITIONAL DATA

The issue of raw material J on 17 May 2007 was for the production of cakes, and that on 28 May 2007 was for the production of biscuits.

The following cost accounting codes are used:

Code number	Description
305	Stock of raw material J
410	Work in progress – cakes
420	Work in progress – biscuits
600	Creditors/purchases ledger control

Task 1.2

Complete the journal below to record separately the FOUR cost accounting entries in respect of the two receipts and two issues during the month of May 2007.

JOURNAL			
Date	Code	Dr (£)	Cr (£)
12 May			
12 May			
17 May			
17 May			
24 May			
24 May			
28 May			
28 May			

ADDITIONAL DATA

The following information relates to direct labour costs incurred in producing 20,000 meat pies during May 2007.

Normal time hours worked	400 hours
Overtime at time and a half worked	80 hours
Overtime at double time worked	60 hours
Total hours worked	540 hours
Normal time hourly rate	£7.50 per hour

Overtime premiums paid are included as part of direct labour cost.

Task 1.3

(a) **Calculate the total cost of direct labour for meat pies for the month of May 2007.**

_____

_____

_____

_____

_____

_____

_____

(b) **Calculate the direct labour cost per meat pie.**

_____

_____

_____

_____

ADDITIONAL DATA

Western Foods Ltd has the following four production departments:

- Baking 1
- Baking 2
- Finishing
- Packaging

The budgeted fixed overheads relating to the four production departments for Quarter 3, 2007 are:

	£	£
Depreciation of fixed assets		70,000
Rent and rates		120,000
Indirect labour costs:		
Baking 1	61,000	
Baking 2	72,500	
Finishing	33,400	
Packaging	20,600	
Total		187,500
Direct packaging costs		20,200
Total fixed overheads		397,700

Fixed overheads are allocated or apportioned to the production departments on the most appropriate basis.

The following information is also relevant:

Department	Net book value of fixed assets (£000)	Square metres occupied	Number of employees
Baking 1	450	650	15
Baking 2	350	550	20
Finishing	400	500	10
Packaging	200	300	7
Total	1,400	2,000	52

Task 1.4

Use the table below to allocate or apportion the fixed overheads between the four production departments, using the most appropriate basis.

Fixed overhead	Basis of allocation or apportionment	Total cost (£)	Baking 1 (£)	Baking 2 (£)	Finishing (£)	Packaging (£)
Depreciation		70,000				
Rent and rates		120,000				
Indirect labour costs		187,500				
Direct packaging costs		20,200				
Totals		397,700				

ADDITIONAL DATA

Baking 1 department recovers its fixed overheads on the basis of the budgeted machine hours. Baking 2 department, however, recovers its fixed overheads on the basis of the budgeted direct labour hours.

The following information relates to these two departments for April 2007.

	Department: Baking 1	Department: Baking 2
Budgeted fixed overhead absorption rate	£40/hour	£30/hour
Actual machine hours worked	1,150	
Actual direct labour hours worked		1,320
Actual fixed overheads	£45,000	£41,000

Task 1.5

(a) **Calculate the fixed overhead absorbed during April 2007 in:**

(i) **the Baking 1 department**

_____

_____

_____

_____

(ii) **the Baking 2 department**

_____

_____

_____

_____

(b) Calculate the over or under absorption (over or under recovery) of fixed overheads during April 2007, stating clearly whether overheads have been over or under absorbed, for:

(i) the Baking 1 department

_____

_____

_____

_____

(ii) the Baking 2 department

_____

_____

_____

_____

ADDITIONAL DATA

The following information relates to the manufacture of batches of birthday cakes during the month of March 2007.

Direct materials per batch	£410.50
Direct labour per batch	£635.40
Total variable overheads	£2,200.00
Total fixed overheads	£3,080.00
Number of batches produced	40

Task 1.6

Calculate the cost per batch of birthday cakes under:

(a)   Variable (marginal) costing

_____

_____

_____

_____

_____

_____

_____

(b)   Full absorption costing

_____

_____

_____

_____

_____

_____

_____

SECTION 2

You should spend about 100 minutes on this section.

Task 2.1

Western Foods Ltd has produced three forecasts of activity levels for the next year for product R, a large premium steak pie. The original budget was to produce only 100,000 units, but production levels of 150,000 units and 200,000 units are also feasible.

(a)   **Complete the table below in order to estimate the production cost per unit (to the nearest penny) of product R at the different activity levels.**

Units made	100,000	150,000	200,000
Costs:	£	£	£
Variable costs:			
• direct materials	75,000		
• direct labour	23,000		
• overheads	18,000		
Fixed costs:			
• indirect labour	8,000		
• overheads	12,000		
Total cost	136,000		
Cost per unit	1.36		

(b)   **Briefly explain how and why the costs per unit of product R change as the level of activity increases.**

_____

_____

_____

_____

(c)   The cost schedule above assumes that all production costs are either variable or fixed.

Briefly explain whether this is realistic. Give ONE example of another way that costs can behave, and provide an example of a type of cost that may behave in this way.

_____

_____

_____

_____

_____

_____

_____

_____

_____

_____

_____

Task 2.2

Products S and T, both speciality cakes, have the following budgeted annual sales and cost information:

Product	S	T
Units made and sold	50,000	75,000
Production hours required	12,500	15,000
Sales revenue (£)	250,000	450,000
Direct materials (£)	90,000	150,000
Direct labour (£)	36,000	48,000
Variable overheads (£)	28,000	27,000

Complete the table below to show the budgeted contribution per unit of S and T sold, and the company's budgeted profit or loss for the year from these two products. Total fixed costs attributable to S and T are budgeted to be £120,000.

	S (£)	T (£)	Total (£)
Unit selling price			
Less: variable costs per unit			
• direct materials			
• direct labour			
• variable overheads			
Contribution per unit			
Sales volume (units)			
Total contribution			
Less: fixed costs			
Budgeted profit or loss			

ADDITIONAL DATA

The £120,000 of fixed costs for products S and T has now been split between the two products as follows: £48,000 to S and £72,000 to T.

The latest sales forecast is for 52,000 units of product S and 75,000 units of product T to be sold during the year.

Task 2.3

(a) **Complete the following table so as to calculate:**

- **the budgeted break-even sales, in units, for each of the two products**
- **the margin of safety (in units) for each of the two products**
- **the margin of safety as a percentage (to two decimal places)**

Product	S	T
Fixed costs (£)		
Unit contribution (£)		
Break-even sales (units)		
Forecast sales (units)		
Margin of safety (units)		
Margin of safety (%)		

(b) Explain the meaning of the term "percentage margin of safety", using your calculations of this figure for products S and T to illustrate your answer.

_____

_____

_____

_____

_____

_____

_____

ADDITIONAL DATA

As a result of refurbishment in the factory, the number of available production hours for products S and T has now been reduced to 25,000 during the year.

Task 2.4

Given this limitation and your calculations from Task 2.2, complete the following table to recommend how many units of products S and T should be made in order to maximise the profits or minimise the loss for the year.

Product	S	T	Total
Contribution/unit (£)			
Production hours/unit			
Contribution/production hr. (£)			
Product ranking			
Production hours available			
Production hours allocated to:			
Product			
Product			
Total contribution earned (£)			
Less: fixed costs (£)			120,000
Profit/loss made (£)			

Task 2.5

Western Foods Ltd is considering introducing a new product, V, for which the following capital expenditure, sales and cost estimates have been produced for its planned three-year product life:

	Year 0 £000	Year 1 £000	Year 2 £000	Year 3 £000
Capital expenditure	160			
Other cash flows:				
Sales income		120	180	240
Operating costs		70	90	110

The company's cost of capital is 10%

Present value (PV) factors for a 10% discount rate are:

	Year 0	Year 1	Year 2	Year 3
PV factor	1.0000	0.9091	0.8264	0.7513

You are required to calculate both the net present value (to two decimal places) and the payback period for the proposed new product V.

(a)   The net present value

	Year 0 £000	Year 1 £000	Year 2 £000	Year 3 £000
Capital expenditure				
Sales income				
Operating costs				
Net cash flows				
PV factors				
Discounted cash flows				
Net present value				

(b)   **The payback period**

_____

_____

_____

_____

_____

_____

_____

_____

Task 2.6

Based on the information given in Task 2.5 and your calculations for this task, write a report to the Management Accountant in which you:

(a)   Recommend, on the basis of both the net present value and the payback period, whether the proposed new product V should be introduced.

(b)   Identify ONE other method of investment appraisal which might also have been used to assess this proposal.

(c)   Identify TWO commercial factors which are also relevant to this decision.

Use the report stationery on the next page.

REPORT

To: The Management Accountant

From:

Subject:

Date:

Practice Examination 5
Premier Pottery Limited

Element coverage

6.1 record and analyse information relating to direct costs and revenues

6.2 record and analyse information relating to the allocation, apportionment and absorption of overhead costs

6.3 prepare and evaluate estimates of costs and revenues

Suggested time allocation

Three hours plus 15 minutes' reading time.

PRACTICE EXAMINATION 5
PREMIER POTTERY LIMITED

This examination is in TWO sections.

You have to show competence in BOTH sections.

You should, therefore, attempt and aim to complete EVERY task in BOTH sections.

Blank space for workings is available on these pages, but all essential workings should be included within your answers, where appropriate.

You should spend about 80 minutes on Section 1 and about 100 minutes on Section 2.

Both sections are based on Premier Pottery Ltd.

DATA

You are employed as an accounting technician with Premier Pottery Ltd, a company that manufactures and sells a range of pottery. Its customers include gift shops, department stores and specialist shops.

You report to the Management Accountant, who has asked you to carry out the following tasks.

SECTION 1

You should spend about 80 minutes on this section.

Task 1.1

The stock record card shown below for type P clay for the month of May 2007 has only been partially completed.

STOCK RECORD CARD FOR TYPE P CLAY								
	Receipts			Issues			Balance	
Date	Quantity	Cost per kg	Total cost	Quantity	Cost per kg	Total cost	Quantity	Total cost
2007	kg	£	£	kg	£	£	kg	£
Balance as at 1 May							4,000	4,800
9 May	2,000	1.35	2,700				6,000	7,500
12 May				1,000	1.25	1,250		
18 May	2,500	1.40						
27 May				3,000				

(a) **Identify the stock issue method being used for valuing issues to production and stocks.**

_____

_____

(b) **Complete the remaining entries in the stock record card using this method.**

ADDITIONAL DATA

The issue of type P clay on 12 May 2007 was for the production of product A, whilst that on 27 May 2007 was for the production of product B.

The following cost accounting codes are used:

Code number	Description
210	Stocks of type P clay
330	Work in progress – Product A
340	Work in progress – Product B
620	Creditors/purchases ledger control

Task 1.2

Complete the journal below to record separately the FOUR cost accounting entries in respect of the two receipts and two issues during the month of May 2007.

JOURNAL			
Date 2007	**Code**	**Dr (£)**	**Cr (£)**
9 May			
9 May			
12 May			
12 May			
18 May			
18 May			
27 May			
27 May			

ADDITIONAL DATA

The following information relates to direct labour costs incurred in producing product C during May 2007.

Normal time hours worked	800 hours
Overtime at time and a half worked	100 hours
Overtime at double time worked	60 hours
Total hours worked	960 hours
Normal time hourly rate	£8 per hour

Task 1.3

Overtime permiums paid are included as part of direct labour costs.

Calculate the total cost of direct labour for product C for the month of May 2007.

_____

_____

_____

_____

_____

_____

_____

_____

ADDITIONAL DATA

Premier Pottery Ltd has the following departments involved in the first stage of production:

- Moulding
- Glazing
- Maintenance

The budgeted fixed overheads relating to the departments for Quarter 3, 2007 are:

	£	£
Insurance of machinery		8,600
Rent and rates		25,400
Indirect labour costs:		
Moulding	88,500	
Glazing	60,200	
Maintenance	20,400	
Total		169,100
Total fixed overheads		203,100

The following information is also available:

Department	Net book value of fixed assets (£000)	Square metres occupied	Number of employees
Moulding	216	315	18
Glazing	108	252	14
Maintenance	36	63	4
Total	360	630	36

Fixed overheads are allocated or apportioned to the departments on the most appropriate basis. The total maintenance overheads are then reapportioned to the two production departments. 60% of the Maintenance department's time is spent maintaining equipment in the Moulding department.

Task 1.4

Use the following table to allocate or apportion the fixed overheads between the production departments, using the most appropriate basis.

Fixed overhead	Basis of allocation or apportionment	Total cost (£)	Moulding (£)	Glazing (£)	Maintenance (£)
Insurance of machinery		8,600			
Rent and rates		25,400			
Indirect labour costs		169,100			
Maintenance		203,100			

ADDITIONAL DATA

Moulding department fixed overheads are absorbed on the basis of machine hours. Glazing department fixed overheads are absorbed on the basis of direct labour hours. The following information relates to the moulding and glazing departments for April 2007.

	Moulding department	*Glazing department*
Budgeted machine hours	2,500	1,350
Budgeted labour hours	3,050	1,800
Budgeted fixed overheads	£38,125	£25,920

Task 1.5

Calculate the budgeted overhead absorption rate for April 2007 for:

(i) the moulding department

_____

_____

_____

_____

(ii) the glazing department

_____

_____

_____

_____

ADDITIONAL DATA

The following information relates to the manufacture of product D during the month of April 2007:

Direct materials per unit	£4.40
Direct labour per unit	£10.20
Total variable overheads	£7,000.00
Total fixed overheads	£5,000.00
Number of units produced	4,000 units

Task 1.6

Calculate the cost per unit of product D under:

(a)   (i)   **Variable (marginal) costing**

_____

_____

_____

_____

_____

_____

_____

(ii)   **Full absorption costing**

_____

_____

_____

_____

_____

_____

_____

(b) **Explain how it is possible to under recover (under absorb) fixed overheads.**

Explanation of fixed overhead under recovery (under absorption):

_____

_____

_____

_____

_____

_____

_____

_____

_____

_____

_____

_____

SECTION 2

You should spend about 100 minutes on this section.

ADDITIONAL DATA

Premier Pottery Ltd has produced three forecasts of activity levels for the next three months for its type E coffee pot. The original budget involved producing 1,000 units, but sales are increasing, and it looks as if production levels of between 1,200 and 1,400 units are now more likely.

Task 2.1

Complete the table below in order to estimate the production cost per unit of the type E coffee pot at the different activity levels.

Units made	1,000	1,200	1,400
Costs:	£	£	£
Variable costs:			
• direct materials	550		
• direct labour	1,250		
• overheads	850		
Fixed costs:			
• indirect labour	600		
• overheads	1,500		
Total cost	4,750		
Cost per unit	4.75		

(b) If the production volume for this product were to increase to 5,000 units per three-month period, explain what the likely effect would be on the fixed costs and cost per unit.

_____

_____

_____

_____

_____

_____

_____

_____

_____

_____

_____

_____

_____

_____

_____

_____

_____

ADDITIONAL DATA

The following budgeted annual sales and cost information relates to pottery products F and G.

Product	F	G
Units made and sold	6,000	10,000
Production hours required	600	2,000
Sales revenue (£)	21,000	50,000
Direct materials (£)	2,400	7,000
Direct labour (£)	3,600	12,000
Variable overheads (£)	3,300	11,000

Total fixed costs attributable to F and G are budgeted to be £16,500.

Task 2.2

Complete the table below (to two decimal places) to show the budgeted contribution per unit of F and G sold, and the company's budgeted profit or loss for the year from these two products.

	F (£)	G (£)	Total (£)
Unit selling price			
Less: variable costs per unit			
• direct materials			
• direct labour			
• variable overheads			
Contribution per unit			
Sales volume (units)			
Total contribution			
Less: fixed costs			
Budgeted profit or loss			

ADDITIONAL DATA

The £16,500 of fixed costs for products F and G has now been split between the two products as follows: £5,850 to F and £10,650 to G.

The latest sales forecast is for 7,000 units of product F and 9,000 units of product G to be sold during the year.

Task 2.3

Complete the following table so as to calculate:

- the budgeted break-even sales, in units, for each of the two products
- the margin of safety (in units) for each of the two products
- the margin of safety as a percentage (to two decimal places)

Product	F	G
Fixed costs (£)		
Unit contribution (£)		
Break-even sales (units)		
Forecast sales (units)		
Margin of safety (units)		
Margin of safety (%)		

ADDITIONAL DATA

As a result of extra maintenance in the factory, the number of available production hours for products F and G has now been reduced to 2,000 during the year.

Task 2.4

Given this limitation and your calculations from Task 2.2, complete the following table to recommend how many units of products F and G should be made in order to maximise the profits or minimise the loss for the year.

Product	F	G	Total
Contribution/unit (£)			
Production hours/unit			
Contribution/production hr. (£)			
Product ranking			
Production hours available			
Production hours allocated to:			
Product			
Product			
Total contribution earned (£)			
Less: fixed costs (£)			16,500
Profit/loss made (£)			

ADDITIONAL DATA

Premier Pottery Ltd is considering introducing a new range of ovenproof cookware. The following estimates of capital expenditure, sales and costs have been produced. The new product range is expected to have a three-year economic life:

	Year 0 £000	Year 1 £000	Year 2 £000	Year 3 £000
Capital expenditure	200			
Other cash flows:				
Sales income		120	220	240
Operating costs		90	130	150

The company's cost of capital is 8%

Present value (PV) factors for an 8% discount rate are:

	Year 0	Year 1	Year 2	Year 3
PV factor	1.0000	0.9259	0.8573	0.7938

Task 2.5

For the proposed new range of cookware, calculate:

(a)   the net present value (to two decimal places)

	Year 0 £000	Year 1 £000	Year 2 £000	Year 3 £000
Capital expenditure				
Sales income				
Operating costs				
Net cash flows				
PV factors				
Discounted cash flows				
Net present value				

(b)   The payback period

_____

_____

_____

_____

_____

_____

_____

_____

Task 2.6

Using the information and your own calculations from Task 2.5, write a report to the Management Accountant in which you:

(a)   Recommend whether the proposed new range of cookware should be introduced.

Note: This should be based on your calculations of the net present value and the payback period.

(b)   Identify TWO commercial factors that are also relevant to this decision.

(c)   Explain the meaning of the term "internal rate of return".

Use the report stationery on the next page.

REPORT

To: The Management Accountant

From:

Subject:

Date:

Appendix:
sample formats

Sample formats include:

- the structure of a total cost statement and a profit statement

- the structure of a manufacturing account and a profit and loss account

- an example of a manufacturing and profit and loss account

APPENDIX - SAMPLE FORMATS

the structure of a total cost statement and a profit statement

TOTAL COST STATEMENT

		£
	Direct materials	x
add	Direct labour	x
add	Direct expenses	x
equals	PRIME COST	x
add	Production overheads	x
equals	PRODUCTION COST	x
add	Selling and distribution costs ┐	x
add	Administration costs ── non-production overheads	x
add	Finance costs ┘	x
equals	TOTAL COST	x

PROFIT STATEMENT

		£
	Sales	x
less	Total cost	x
equals	PROFIT	x

the structure of a manufacturing account and a profit and loss account

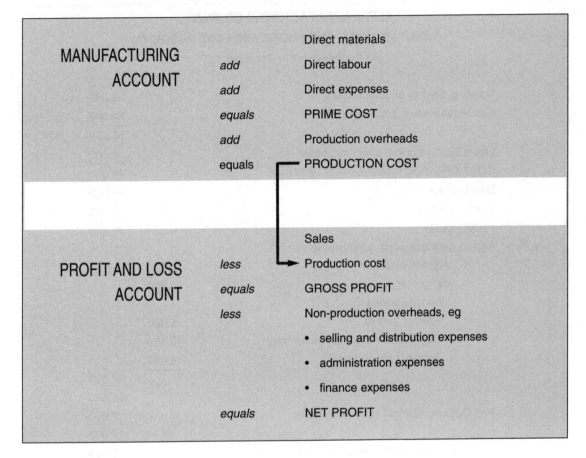

an example of a manufacturing and profit and loss account

ALPHA MANUFACTURING COMPANY
MANUFACTURING AND PROFIT AND LOSS ACCOUNT
for the year ended 31 December 2007

	£	£
Opening stock of direct materials		5,000
Add Purchases of direct materials		50,000
		55,000
Less Closing stock of direct materials		6,000
COST OF DIRECT MATERIALS USED		49,000
Direct labour		26,000
Direct expenses		2,500
PRIME COST		77,500
Add Production (factory) overheads:		
Indirect materials	2,000	
Indirect labour	16,000	
Indirect expenses:		
Rent of factory	5,000	
Depreciation of factory machinery	10,000	
Factory light and heat	4,000	
		37,000
		114,500
Add Opening stock of work-in-progress		4,000
		118,500
Less Closing stock of work-in-progress		3,000
PRODUCTION COST OF GOODS COMPLETED		115,500
Sales		195,500
Opening stock of finished goods	6,500	
Production cost of goods completed	115,500	
	122,000	
Less Closing stock of finished goods	7,500	
COST OF SALES		114,500
Gross profit		81,000
Less Non-production overheads:		
Selling and distribution expenses	38,500	
Administration expenses	32,000	
Finance expenses	3,500	
		74,000
Net profit		7,000